The Blessings and Bling

How Faith and Fashion Helped Me Survive Breast Cancer

Dr. Sheron Patterson

Scripture quotations, unless otherwise noted, are taken
from the Holy Bible, New International Version®, NIV®.
Copyright © 1973, 1978, 1984 by Biblica, Inc.™ Used by
permission of Zondervan. All rights reserved worldwide.
www.zondervan.com

Edited by RootSky Books
www.rootskybooks.com

Cover photo by Kwaunane Burton Photography
Dress courtesy of ooh la la Boutique, Grapevine, TX
Illustrations on pages 51, 57, 91 by Jaron McGlover

First Edition

Printed in the United States of America

This book is dedicated to the
millions of women around the world
who battle breast cancer

Contents

Acknowledgments

I have been blessed to be a blessing. I thank God for ongoing opportunities to bless others. This book would not be possible without my parents William and Johnsie Covington who took me to church every Sunday. I thank my husband Robert Patterson for unconditional love and support during the scariest years of my life. I thank my sons Robby and Chris for accepting me as mom, whether I had cancer or not.

I thank my dynamic duo of doctors,my breast cancer doctor Dr. Michael Grant and my plastic surgeon Dr. David Morales. Hats off to my gynecologist, Dr. Lisa King who made it all happen. Dr. King, thank you for forcing me to get an annual mammogram, even thought I felt fine.

I thank Methodist Health System for finding the cancer in my left breast even though I had an attitude about it. I also thank Methodist Health System for partnering with me to create the Patterson Pledge. Together we changed lives of many women. I thank Baylor Hospitals of Dallas for excellent health care, and partnerships on programs.

I thank Highland Hills UMC for supporting me before, during and after my breast cancer journey. This is a very loving congregation.

I thank Highland Park UMC for continued financial support of my breast cancer ministry and underwriting Breast Cancer Builds. I thank Habitat for Humanity for the opportunity to partner and launch my gratitude project Breast Cancer Builds. I salute all the women,men and young adults who helped build the two houses.

Thanks to Parkland Hospital and Methodist Health System for partnering with me to launch Mammograms for the Masses and providing free mammograms to low income or no income women.

I am indebted to all of the Dallas/Fort Worth radio and television stations, as well as local newspapers and magazines. I especially appreciate the coverage given to me by the

Channel 4 television. They produced numerous segments that followed my journey from diagnosis to surgery and helped many people to face their fears about cancer. Thank you to anchors Shaun Rabb and anchor Clarice Tinsely.

I am deeply grateful to The Dallas Morning News for supporting my mission to help as many people as I could by writing my story. This book is based on the columns that I wrote for The Dallas Morning News.

Thanks to a host ofgirlfriends, guy friends, pastors and clergy sisters who supported and prayed for me,the Dallas Summit, Spelman College class of 1981 and the members of Delta Sigma Theta Sorority.

I thank the Dallas Women's Foundation, for helping get my nonprofit off the ground, and the Community Council of Greater Dallas for assisting with the nonprofit.

Thanks to the American Cancer Society, The Komen for the Cure Foundation , Baker Bots Law firm for legal services and the, Strasburg and Price Law firm for saluting my breast cancer projects

I thank my glam squad who work overtime to keep me looking good. Thanks to the very talented photographers who helped present me to the public.

Finally, I thank the vast numbers of people, that I do not know, who prayed for me during my breast cancer journey. Your prayers carried me. Truly, **"The effective, fervent prayer of a righteous man avails much." James 5:16**

Introduction

They say that "the Lord moves in mysterious ways," and I am a witness — a fashionably dressed witness, that is. My faith and my interest in fashion converged to help me through one of the toughest times of my life — my bout with breast cancer.

I have my priorities straight. I love God. I love teaching, preaching and studying God's Word. I also happen to like bling. (A rhinestone here and there never hurt anybody.) I like to shop and dress as fashionably as I can without blowing the mortgage on an outfit. My love and my like helped me survive breast cancer. I learned that with a strong faith and a chic outfit, I could make it — along with gifted physicians and the marvels of modern medicine and technology!

Faith and fashion is an amazing combination.

God cannot be limited to one section of who we are. God is present in both our outer and inner lives, and should be recognized and celebrated in both areas. The greatness of faith and the glamour of fashion are a perfect duo for surviving breast cancer. The two are intertwined in my life. God is in all of it.

Allow me to offer a Sheron remix on Psalm 139:7: "Where can I go from your Spirit? If I go to the shoe department, you are there, or to the jewelry counter, you are there." God is with us all the time and everywhere, and it is a good thing.

Fashion mimics God's creation. The color palettes of a designer's fall collection or a makeup line's eye shadow and lip-gloss are humanity's attempt to mirror all of God's glory. Take me, for example. The python print on the 4-inch pumps on my feet represents God's majestically hued creature — the snake. The deep purple-colored pantsuit on my body pays homage to the vegetable direct from God's hand — the eggplant.

Faith lives and breathes because of God's track record of goodness. So says **Psalm 124:1: "If the Lord had not been on our side, where would we be?"** My faith enables me to write about my blessed breast cancer journey because I want to tell the world how powerful God is in all ways. A ministry grew out of my misery. A purpose grew out of my pain. I thought breast cancer would be the end; it was my launching pad for life. I never thought I would say it, but the breast cancer was a blessing.

Faith and fashion will not keep you from the challenges of breast cancer. I am not writing naïve fairy tales to lull you into the falsehoods that your health journey will be trouble-free because of your relationship with Jesus or the latest pair of jeans. Reading this book does not guarantee that you will outlive the cancer in your body. Your hair may fall out due to the chemotherapy. The radiation treatments may burn your skin. Your cancer surgery site may become infected and require additional work. The stress and strain of the cancer may chase away family and friends. But I am here to tell you that a strong relationship with Jesus enables you to withstand the pain and praise God anyhow. Also, looking good, as you are going through, helps the situation. You can endure with the peace of God inside and a swank outfit on the outside. The truly well coordinated woman has both.

I am many things. I am a Christian clotheshorse, a faithful fashionista, a grateful glamour girl. I am a wife, mother, daughter, friend and ordained United Methodist pastor. I am a cancer survivor with a story to tell. If you or someone you know is battling cancer, allow my story to encourage and inspire. As you read this, laugh, cry, think, pray and realize that there is more than one way to fight cancer. Depression and fear seized me. I learned I had to choose how I would respond to my problems. You can, too. Attitude is everything — along with the right outfit.

I will help you make lemonade from your lemons; make Kool-Aid out of your cancer, and make Popsicles out of your problems. I am not trying to minimize the severity of your situation, but I want to emphasize that God is bigger than whatever is going wrong in your life. Instead of running to God to report how big your problems are, run to the problem and tell it how big our God is. When cancer-related blues hit you, send up a prayer and reach in your closet to put on your sharpest outfit. Then strut like you know God will make a way. God has given me "**... a crown of beauty instead of ashes, the oil of joy instead of mourning, and a garment of praise instead of a spirit of despair." Isaiah 61:3**

CHAPTER 1
Bargain Shopper

eals. Rebates. Clearances. Coupons. This is the lingo of the typical bargain shopper, and yes, I rarely can resist a good sale. This time I was a different type of bargain shopper. I bargained for my life. It was the middle of winter and it was cold outside. Yet I was in the stores looking at spring and summer clothes. This was hard work because winter clothes were everywhere. A gorgeous charcoal gray, cashmere sweater called my name, while a cranberry-colored wool coat with big gold buttons winked at me from the racks. But I did not pause to admire them, try them on or buy them. I purchased spring and summer clothes day after day after day. I bought linen blouses in canary yellow and sky blue. The next time, I bought an outrageous orange terry cloth bathing suit cover-up. The time after that, I bought high heeled and flat sandals in metallic hues and belts to match. I was ready for the seasons to change. My challenge was living long enough to wear them.

I was not interested in resort wear. I was a woman with a fresh cancer diagnosis caught up in desperation. A breast cancer diagnosis invaded my life, and I experienced desperation like never before. I was new to this and unsure how long I had to live. I knew lots of women who had died from breast cancer. I was very afraid and very sad. Some people turned to drugs and alcohol when they faced crisis. I turned to Christ and clothes. They were my old standbys. I heard that mood–boosting things happen when shoppers like me hit the stores. The neurotransmitter dopamine gets released and it provides a good feeling, a high of sorts.

Before cancer, I shopped for pleasure and dressed up to please myself. With cancer, I shopped to survive. I shopped to keep my mind off breast cancer. Most of my days were spent anywhere they sold women's clothes and accessories. The more, the better, because variety is the spice of life and this spice had me high. I flocked from high-end couture boutiques to discount stores in strip shopping malls. Clothes are clothes. I loved them all. They loved me back and were happy to see my car pull into a parking spot at the boutique, outlet mall or strip shopping center. Or at least, I told myself that.

I dressed up to cover up my rapidly descending countenance. One day, head-to-toe winter white — from the boots on my feet to the beret on my head. The next day I wore a chocolate wool suit, with a coordinated silk blouse underneath. I looked great on the outside. The beautiful clothes did their job of covering up my hurt. I clung to words of encouragement such as **2 Corinthians 4:16: "Therefore we do not lose heart. Though outwardly we are wasting away, yet inwardly we are being renewed day by day."**

Sometimes I felt better. Sometimes I did not.

I made religious pilgrimages to the shrines called clothing stores several times a week. I felt like some type of Old Testament prophet standing in the temple with a slain dove or a goat on the altar ready for sacrifice. The shoes, clothes and purses were offerings of sort to God. Standing over the racks of clothes, I cut many a deal with God right in the middle of the women's clothing department.

Deep down inside of my faith, I concocted a private, insane, one-sided bargain with God. For the record, God never co-signed on this, but I kept putting it out there just in case God decided that I was worthy, and that I should be allowed to live. In the classic descriptions of the stages of grief, I was in the third stage — bargaining. (Hey, speaking of classics — don't you just love a crisp navy blue blazer in the spring? Or how about the ever-classic white cotton shirt? I am always on the hunt for the ultimate white shirt with timeless sleeves, collar and cuffs.)

I bargained with God on every clothing purchase. "God," I pleaded, "if you allow me to buy this dress, please allow me to live long enough to wear it." I had the faith to envision myself in the spring, healthy and happy. I prayed that the piles of clothes tilted the balance in my favor for a change. "God, if I buy this floral print sun dress, will I live long enough to wear it? Surely God — you know how good I would look in this white cotton blazer and matching slacks in June and July. If you let me buy it can I wear it?"

I whispered these prayers to God because I was too afraid to pray the traditional way. You know, the "thy will be done on earth as it is in heaven," traditional prayer. I did not pray traditionally because I did not want a traditional answer. I wanted God to do something awesome and amazing. I had the audacity to pray out of the box. Shopping for the next season's clothes was my prayer language.

The sales clerks were my congregation. They were friend-ly, warm and had no relationship to my cancer. The clerks did not know my diagnosis. We did not discuss cancer treat-ments. They did not know that I was frantically trying to save my life. I appeared like any other woman buying clothes, but I was in dialogue with God the whole time. In the stores I did not feel like a woman who had breast cancer and a doubtful future. I felt normal, healthy and hopeful in the stores. Shop-ping gave me a new identity — anonymous and cancer-free.

At the end of many days, I drove home with the trunk of my car crammed with shopping bags. I felt good, because the more bags I had, the longer I would live. I prayed.

This entire breast cancer journey started one December morning, when I was supposed to go shopping at the mall.

CHAPTER 2
Mall Detour

On that December morning, I was supposed to be at one of the mega-malls shopping for Christmas gifts. Christmas was just around the corner, and there were presents to purchase. I was one of those who seemed drawn by a magnetic force to the overcrowded shopping center. It was just one of those things you do, in addition to drinking eggnog and decorating a Christmas tree.

For the record, though, I do not like December shopping or any holiday-related shopping, for that matter. The malls and highways that lead to the malls are crazy-crowded. I prefer the quiet, zen-like calm of shopping off-holiday, mid-morning when the stores are tranquil, clean and empty. I have the sales clerks and the stores all to myself. That December, I tolerated the crowds and pressed my way inward to handle my business. My hands were on the steering wheel, guiding my car on the highway entrance ramp when I suddenly remembered, "My mammogram is scheduled for today." So I delayed my shopping for what should have been 45 minutes, to quickly get my annual mammogram, and get back on task.

I had a mammogram performed every year. They were not a big deal. It was an in-and-out process. Lots of women make a big deal out of mammograms. On a pain scale of 1 to 10, I'd give them a 7. They are a necessary pain. We women undergo lots of other painful procedures like waxes and weaves. Some diets are painful: you want to eat the cake and you can't.

I entered the mammography center, and signed in with the attendant. I had shopping to do, so I was glad someone called my name rather quickly and assigned me to a small cubicle to change and wait. Mammogram wear is something to behold. Mine was a baby blue, snap enclosure, cape type of garment. I was never good with capes, ponchos and other types of hanging clothes that drape the body. I never knew the front from the back, and I felt like a hanger. I made the most of this fashion disaster. I removed my shirt and bra and put on the cape. Then, once my name was called, I walked down the hall to the mammogram machine like I was walking the runway of a New York fashion week show, and the cape I was wearing was direct from Milan. Why not have fun in life? Make the most of whatever you have on! *If I can't wear this mammogram cape with panache — who can?*

One-two-three. Smash. Right breast. One-two-three. Smash. Left breast. I sucked up the momentary pain. I returned to my cubicle to change clothes and get to the mall. I dressed in a flash. *They'll be calling my name and sending me out of here any second,* I thought. A second came and went. I picked up one of the magazines in my cubicle and glanced at it half-heartedly. I refused to start reading the good articles because I would not be there long enough to finish them. Time passed.

When I realized I had finished two good articles in the magazine, I got angry. "These people have forgotten I am in here," I steamed. "I am going to find the attendant to let her know that my mammogram film was okay."

My mammogram film had always been okay. I should have been on my way to the mall already.

I flung the cubicle door open with the frustration of a woman kept waiting too long. Standing in front of me was the attendant, about to knock on the door. She said, "We need to take another mammogram. It's probably nothing, but the radiologist needs another angle of your breast."

At that moment, fear descended on me. It jumped down my throat and took up residence inside me. Somehow I knew something was wrong. I knew this would not be a routine second trip back to the mammography machine. I did not buy the "it's probably nothing" routine. Not for one minute. *That's just the line they feed you to coax you back to the machine.*

I wanted to run out of the cubicle. I wanted to sprint out of the mammography center so fast that I could break one of those track and field records set at the Olympics. The sight of me moving down the street with the mammogram cape flapping in the wind was laughable. But I was not laughing. I did not want a gold medal, I just wanted to be told, "Everything is fine, and you can go home. See you next year."

Running away was useless. I obliged and returned to the

machine. It was no fashion show runway this time. My steps were not light. They were labored and heavy, like the character in a scene from *The Green Mile*, when he was heading down death row. I felt like a dead woman walking toward the gas chamber.

The second round of mammograms yielded results that no one wants to hear, "We've found something on your film."

After I dressed, I was led to a dark room where a radiologist guy sat surrounded by illuminated screens that held mammogram films of a host of breasts. Some were large. Some were small. I assumed mine were somewhere up there. He pointed to the screen to his left. On it were the contents of my left breast. "I found something right here," he said.

"I don't see anything," I challenged him. I squinted and placed my nose close to the lit board.

Since I could not see anything, maybe he would come to his senses and say, "Oops, sorry, I had your film mixed up with someone else."

Besides, can't he look at me and see that I am healthy and have no health issues? I reasoned.

"There," he said, pointing to tiny, microscopic, white specks. I was both indignant and amazed at his discovery. I was indignant at the thought that something irregular had been found in me. I harbored a secret, elite mentality about my health. I thought I was invincible. My parents were in their 70s and in excellent health. I was 47 and felt as healthy as a horse. I never missed a day of school as a kid. (Part of the perfect attendance was due to very good health, and the other to a mother who was a schoolteacher and believed that I was never too sick for school.)

This radiologist guy burst my illusion bubble. I was shot down. There was no warning for this illness. Shouldn't my body have warned me that these white, microscopic specks existed before now? I could not believe I was standing there discussing a potential health problem.

Even though I felt strong when I walked into that place, I felt weak and vulnerable.

Softly, reluctantly I conceded defeat to this radiologist

guy whom I started to dislike intensely. "Yes, I see them."

It is quite a feat to detect these minute specks, I admitted to myself. I was not ready to congratulate this guy I planned to dislike. He had the potential to launch me on a journey toward cancer, and I was not having that. I should have been praising God that this man had the keen eyesight to see the specks, rather than wanting to slap him silly for seeing what I did not want found.

"It's probably nothing," he reiterated. "It is not at all uncommon to find calcifications in the milk ducts. Since these are so small, you probably have nothing to worry about. Here are your two options: Come back in six months and we will check their status. Or, have a biopsy."

"What is a biopsy?" I asked.

"It's a procedure that samples tissue from the area of the specks."

Quickly I deduced that any sampling of tissues meant blood and pain in my breast. Neither one of these were on my list of things to get done, so my answer was clear. "I will check back with you in six months. Thank you. Goodbye."

I was off the hook. I congratulated myself. "Pretty smooth," I smirked. I ended this brush with cancer quickly and quietly. After all, I had shopping to get done. Now I was off to face the crazy crowds and highways.

CHAPTER 3

Biopsy In Basic Black

very wardrobe, according to the experts, should revolve
around a few garments in basic black. The little black
dress, a black blazer and a black pair of slacks. Black is
the quintessential neutral that brings all the other garments
together in fashion harmony. I followed the fashion rules,
and dutifully had the above in my closet. The pieces worked
wonderfully. What I also now had was unwanted — basic
black marks on my breast, compliments of a biopsy. I had
not dodged the biopsy after all.

My attempts at denial failed. A few days after the visit to
the mammography center, I received a phone call from a local hospital that informed me a biopsy was scheduled for me
in early January. My gynecologist scheduled it. *How dare
she make assumptions about my life?* Remind me to find
another gynecologist. Preferably one who does not butt into
her patient's life. If I wanted to wait on those specks, I would
wait. They were my specks. I was incensed.

The pressure of the upcoming biopsy and the lack of
knowledge about the specks put a pall on Christmas for me.
People were singing *Joy to the World* and I was running from
the world. I wanted to hide in a cave, or find a huge rock to
curl up under. I thought maybe people could look at me and
see that something was wrong. I did not want to celebrate
anything. I did not care that Jesus was the reason for the
season. How could I care? I might have breast cancer, and
I might die.

Biopsies are not nice, at all. Yes, they are a necessary
part of medical science. They enable doctors to determine
what is going on inside our bodies. But I was not thrilled to
be in a hospital about to be biopsied. The two women — a
doctor and a nurse — guided me through the procedure.
They tried their best to be kind. Their smiles were distrac-
tions for me. They spoke in very pleasant tones and made me
feel like I just walked into a tea party. Why were they so nice?
They compensated for the hell they put me through, all in the
name of retrieving a sample of the tissue. They described the
procedure in a matter-of-fact way, but it was not. I wished
getting a sample of tissue was as easy as getting a urine or

blood sample. In actuality it was a procedure that seemed to me like a space age torture experience. Surely the *Alien* or another extraterrestrial villain was behind a curtain in this biopsy room choreographing my agony. I lay on my stomach on a table with a circle in it, large enough for my left breast to dangle through. The dangling breast was compressed to its thinnest point by a cruel machine. (Imagine a mammogram machine on steroids.) Excruciating pain covered me. To increase the suffering, a thick, hollow needle was inserted deep into my flesh. The goal was to extract a small amount of breast tissue that held the white specks. The problem was that the tissue that contained the specks was not on the surface, but deep in the center of my breast.

I quivered with pain from head to toe when the needle bored into my flesh. "Hold still please," the women asked softly. I complied and heard a grinding sound. It was the sound of my flesh being extracted from my breast. It sickened me to listen, but I remained motionless in order to complete this gruesome process.

The grinding stopped. The needle was pulled out of my breast. "We need to examine this sample under a microscope in the next room," they said. "Don't move."

I nodded. *How can I move?* My breast was clamped like a pancake and I was suspended upside down.

They left me to entertain myself. I prayed.

I whimpered. I prayed. I whimpered.

They returned with bad news. The white specks moved. The friendly women did not get any of the white specks with the first extraction. They wanted to repeat the process. The second round was like the first, but I lost what cool I thought I had. My body shook as I anticipated the burning sensation of the needle. When it plunged into my flesh, I recoiled. My whole body shuddered from side to side like shaken Jell-O on a plate.

"You moved. You moved," the women chastised me. "We probably did not get the proper sample this time either." They pulled the needle out of my flesh and examined it under a microscope. I waited again, clamped down and suspended. I felt like one of those big pieces of meat that hung in a butcher's freezer.

The intense pain made me angry and defiant. The women returned with more bad news. The white specks were not captured. But they had good news too. "There are no other patients after you, Sheron, so we have all day to keep trying."

Without batting an eye, I spoke as fiercely as one can who is clamped down and suspended. "You two may have all day, but you have one more chance to get it right with me. If you miss the white specks this third time, let me out of this contraption. I don't care if I have breast cancer or not."

The white specks were finally captured on the third try. Once the kind women released me from the machinery I burst into tears. I cried because of the pain. I cried because I was furious that I found myself in this ordeal. I was healthy. There was nothing wrong with me. Three days later I received two phone calls — one from the doctor who performed the biopsy, the other from my gynecologist. They both said the same thing. "We are sorry to tell you this, but you have breast cancer."

My fears had been substantiated. I turned to what I knew best in a time of trouble — prayer and fasting. If I could pray over the clothes racks in the stores like an Old Testament prophet, couldn't I pray now? Unlike the bargaining I did in the store, prayer and fasting were not concocted by me, nor were they insane. God has co-signed on these. Jesus said, **"This kind can come forth by nothing but by prayer and fasting." Mark 9: 29 KJV**

Prayer and fasting are a part of my spiritual practices. The same way I adhere to a host of fashion principles such as the old-fashioned habit of wearing slips with sheer garments, I also adhere to prayer and fasting. These are foundations that keep me going. Prayer and fasting are ancient practices that tie us close to God. The truth is, as much as I enjoy looking good on the outside, the practices keep me looking good on the inside, and that is most important.

I turned to these to keep me from going over the edge.

Some people think you have to pray at a special place and say special words. Sometimes when I was completely decimated by the thoughts of the unknown, all I could do was to call on the name of Jesus. I am convinced that His name alone has power to turn situations around. In the Bible the name of Jesus brought forth miracles. Surely the same was true for me.

I do not have a prayer closet. That's a special place some people have, complete with an altar, pillows and Bibles. I turned whatever space I was in, into my prayer closet. It could be a dressing room in a store or the waiting room at a doctor's office.

My prayers, like the ones in the clothing stores, were aggressive. I was never one for weak-kneed, puny prayers. I prayed the scriptures back to God. I have been told that God likes to hear us speak the scriptures with confidence. If God likes it, I like it.

"God, you said that no weapon formed against me shall prevail," I prayed, recalling **Isaiah 54:17.**

I continued, "God, you said, 'Call Me, and I will answer you.' Lord, you said that you will be with me in trouble. And that you will deliver me. You said that you will satisfy me fully with long life, and I will see your salvation. God, I am standing on your word right now because there is nothing else."

•

I prayed these in God's face type prayers for the rest of the journey.

It was time to get serious with God. My life was at stake. Fasting is what I do when I really want to get God's attention, and I certainly did it then.

•

Fasting from food occurs when I really know that I am in trouble. After I have prayed and meditated, and still nothing occurs, that's when I turn over my plate. When I give up food and choose to fill up my spirit with the word of God, God then does something with me. The key about being a person of faith is realizing that we often want God to do some-

29

thing about our situation, when we really need to ask God to change us. That's what happened to me. Fasting was not easy. I was hungry for food, but I was hungrier for God's movement in my life. People around me ate, but I sipped on bottled water. I ignored the growling stomach and focused on my growing faith.

I wanted God to do something in my life. Healing of course, but more than that, I wanted to feel the presence and power of God as I walked through the cancer journey. I got tired of relying on self and clothes. They were no longer enough. Something on the inside needed to show up on the outside. I declared a fast. I went without food for five days. It was liquids only. What was I thinking? I am the queen of breakfast, lunch and dinner — with a healthy snack of fruit or Greek yogurt in between. Fast? Surely there was another way to hear from God and come up out of this funk.

Day one was the hardest. I was angry with myself for setting such a high goal. I wrestled with my flesh, and its desire to eat. *A turkey burger sounds good right about now, I thought as I looked ahead to five days of not eating. God if you are going to do something, can you do it now? So I can eat?*

Day two was hard as well. I had hunger headaches. I was highly irritated and grouchy. It was difficult to put on a smile and function in society. *Lord, speak to me.*

Day three was a turning point. It was not so difficult to go without food. The times in prayer filled me up and instead of worrying about what I could not eat; I got excited about what God could do.

Day four was the day I learned to get out of the way to allow God to truly take control of this situation. Fear had taken residence for far too long. As I filled up on God, there was less of me.

Day five was the best day. I was full of the spirit of God, and my mind was in a happy, peaceful place. My body felt ready to take on whatever was ahead. I felt prepared.

•

The praying and fasting prepared me to walk into a strange

place where I did not belong. It all seemed like I was in the wrong place at the wrong time. Surely this was somebody else's situation.

CHAPTER 4
The Wrong Dressing Room

Women have comical experiences in the dressing rooms of stores. One woman was trying on pants, lost her balance and fell through the curtain of the dressing room and onto the floor of the show room, where everyone saw her half-dressed. Another woman tried on a dress that was too small, got it stuck over her head, and was too embarrassed to call for help. I wished I could have laughed off the experience I was having. It was like walking into the wrong dressing room and seeing someone else's clothes hanging there. That's what it felt like when I walked into the cancer doctor's office for the first time. I wanted to turn around and find the place I was supposed to be. Certainly not there.

I eyed the other women who were sitting with me in the waiting room, and I wanted to let them know that I really should not be there. I wanted them to understand that was the first and last time they would see me in the waiting room, so there was no need to get used to seeing me.

In the examination room the doctor listened as I eagerly complained about the tortuous biopsy I endured. I hoped that as he applied pressure to my breasts and lymph nodes, he too would say, "Sheron, there is no cancer here. You are healthy as a horse. Why don't you go on home and quit taking up my valuable time?"

I held out hope that I could go home and forget this incident ever happened.

Instead, the doctor asked me to get dressed and meet him in the library of his office to review my biopsy results and discuss my future. I became anxious. I started to shake standing there. These were warnings from my senses that bad news was coming. I brought a notebook and pen along to record what the doctor said. I believed that they made me appear in control and intelligent. But once the doctor sat down and detailed my situation, the ability to write or even comprehend evaporated.

"You have ductal carcinoma in situ," he said. This meant that the cancer was not moving beyond the breast ducts. It was not aggressive nor was it invasive. "You have two choices. You can get a lumpectomy, followed by 33 sessions of radiation, or a mastectomy."

At this point, the room started to spin and I felt limp. I wanted to faint, pass out or do something just to escape the reality before me. I did not want a lumpectomy or radiation! And who in their right mind wanted a breast removed?

I was angry that a mastectomy was even offered to me. It was cruel and inappropriate to speak the word mastectomy to a woman who thought she was healthy. Anger and fear rose to the surface and sprung out in the form of tears. In the midst of tears and sobs I responded, "I don't want either option."

As if I had a choice.

The pen and paper were abandoned. I thought if I cried hard enough, the doctor would give me a different diagnosis. Wrong. In the midst of my wailing, it dawned on me that the doctor knew that I was a pastor. My meltdown may have shocked him. Perhaps he assumed that when clergy received a notice that they could either have a breast radiated or removed, they broke out in a verse of *Kum Ba Yah*. Not me, and not now.

In an unexpected twist, the doctor graciously assumed my role and offered me scriptural reassurances. "Perhaps God has a reason for this. Maybe you are to help other women," he said softly.

"Help other women?" I snarled. "I can't even help myself."

What I refused to hear with my head, I heard with my heart. I stored that word of promise and power inside and it grew. God spoke in my chaos. God is always speaking to us. Even at our lowest, most painful moments, God speaks. Even when we are in the wrong fitting room and have to try on someone else's clothes, God speaks. The challenge I faced was in understanding what was about to happen.

I prayed, "God you said that I should be still, and know that you are God. So I am standing still to hear from you."

The problem was, as I waited, my fear had grown to floor-length proportions.

CHAPTER 5

Floor-Length Fear

There is something chic about floor-length clothes. Every now and then I donned long garments because I felt regal with all the fabric swirling about. Even if it was a long denim dress or a Matrix-looking coat, floor-length anything made me feel like I owned the place. Sadly, my fear was taking on greater lengths, too. It grew from a mini to a maxi with a 50-foot train. I allowed negative thoughts to capture me. My mind was held hostage to questions like:

"How much time do I have left?"

"Will I get to see my children grow up?"

"Will I be disfigured by the surgery?"

"Will I lose my hair to chemotherapy?"

"Will my husband reject me? Or be repelled by how I look?"

"Can I afford the surgery and on-going treatment costs?"

"Will my friends be there for me?"

"Will I be able to hold on to my job?"

"Will I ever be happy again?"

"Will I lose my interest in fashion?"

"Will I be in too much pain to care how I look?"

Cancer was nothing to play with, dismiss or downplay. I knew a host of women and men who had died from it. Who was I to think I would be different? Breast cancer produced fear because it is such a formidable foe. Annually some 40,000 women die from it. Each year 200,000 women receive the life-altering news that cancer has been detected in their breasts and fear covers them like a blanket. I know that fear.

I have been afraid before. I was afraid that I had accidentally worn white after Labor Day. I was afraid that one of my favorite shoe stores had sold the final pair of 9½ pumps that I adored but could not afford at the time. I was afraid to wear pearls and chains together when the trend first emerged. But this fear was something new.

Fear is a feeling of agitation and anxiety. It is when you sense apprehension in your gut. Worry, terror, fright, horror and dread are forms of fear. Everyone is afraid of something — the dark, heights, a relationship or even success. Fear, some say is the most powerful of all emotions. The body demonstrates fear with tense muscles, clenched teeth, raised blood pressure, and the release of stress hormones. All of that described me.

Fear can overcome the body and shut it down. A dangerous stiffness spreads and the body is paralyzed. In the jungle when a lion appears out of nowhere, the antelope is transfixed, forgetting about sprinting off. He gets eaten. In the jungles of our world, many lions prowl, leaving us too frightened to move. Our imaginations are the lion's best friends. If left unchecked, the imaginations feed our fears.

My head pounded. My stomach churned. All my beautiful clothes seemed ill-fitting and drab. Nothing fit right or felt right.

Where was my faith and fashion at this time? Honestly, I laid them both down beside me on my bed of affliction. I was overwhelmed. I reminded the Lord of his words of **Psalm 40:2: "You said you would draw me up from the desolate pit, out of the miry bog."**

From this low state I remembered another time that fear had rendered me to my lowest; a shopping excursion in Beijing went terribly wrong. I shopped way beyond the allotted time given by the stern bus driver. He said, "Be back on this bus by 3 p.m. or you will be left."

I took him seriously, but I was finding marvelous items when I noticed it was way past 4. Fear took over me as I realized that I was abandoned in Beijing. Fear overwhelmed me and knocked me to the sidewalk in front of the stores I had shopped in.

Arms loaded with shopping bags, I wiped away tears that flowed like rivers from my eyes. I did not speak Chinese, and had no clue how to find my tour group. I sobbed for what seemed like hours. I was not sure, but a still, small voice spoke to me and said, "Fool, get up!"

And I did get up. I wiped my tears and heard scriptures rising up out of me.

"The Lord is my light and my salvation." Psalm 27: 1

"Cast all your anxiety on him because he cares for you." 1 Peter 5:7

"I can do everything through him who gives me strength." Philippians 4:13.

Somehow those powerful words put my feet into action and soon I was walking around the area, quoting scripture, totally at peace with my situation. I looked up and around the corner, and the bus was coming to look for me.

That same still voice returned to me again with the same message, as I lay in bed following my cancer diagnosis. I responded the same way. It took me a little while, but I got up, got over my situation and started moving forward. One thing I did know was that I always had choices. I chose which pair of shoes to wear each day, and I could certainly choose which emotion I would let run wild in my life. Fear and depression were choices — uninvited choices. They could be escorted off the premises. Some people need help getting rid of these two. Maybe I would too, but for now I decided to get up and face this thing head-on. There was a God behind me and clothes on me — whom shall I fear?

I had a good friend who had just come through breast cancer. Surely she would help me.

CHAPTER 6

Fashion Friend

The word "mastectomy" hung over my head like a 50-ton weight. I turned to my fashion friend Beverly to help me carry this load. A fashion friend is invaluable. A girl can't have too many friends who share her sense of style and fashion. A fashion friend is one to talk trends with and give honest opinions about whether the dress is too tight and whether the pants make you look fat. A fashion friend who dresses well and loves the Lord is a double blessing. I had one in Beverly. We are sisters in bling.

I was terrified at the possibility of losing one of my breasts. I underwent a lumpectomy and expected that this relatively minimal surgery would remove the cancer. A lumpectomy removes the cancer when it is located in a targeted area. Mine was a two-surgery procedure. The first half was excruciating. Wires were inserted deep into my breast to identify the area to be removed during the lumpectomy. The second half was a breeze because I was unconscious.

Even though my breast was very sore, bandaged and a bit bloody, I was one step closer to getting this cancer out of my body. Once the surgery was over, I was grateful all that required of me was a little lump of breast flesh. I was ready to get back to life as normal. I could live with scars on one of my breasts. It is a small price, and I gladly paid it.

Beverly had been down this road. She was a recent breast cancer survivor and she survived with style and grace. She was my fashion friend and my role model on many levels: fashion, career and overall guts. This woman can dress. Her sense of style is unmatched. From the cut of her hair to the polish on her nails and the heels of her leather stilettos — she is fashion and poise. She is never over the top, but high on the mark. Beverly is an executive and when she walks into a room her wardrobe says that she means business. She does not even have to open her mouth; her clothes say it all. The best news is that when she does open her mouth — pure knowledge and power comes out.

I admire Beverly greatly because she has overcome many obstacles in life in addition to the breast cancer. She was born poor, and pretty much raised herself because her parents were uncaring. Beverly married young and married wrong. She looked up one day and realized she was hitched to a guy who did not care about her or their three children. Armed with her powerful will and not much else, she struck out for the big city of Dallas. There she got an education, raised her daughters and ran a profitable business for many years. A wonderful husband was the one thing that eluded her, and when she met Ed, she knew he was it. They were both 60 when they wed and I was delighted to co-officiate their Christmas wedding.

•

Cancer is cold-blooded. It does not care that you have found the love of your life and everything is mapped out wonderfully. A cancerous, stage 3 lump suddenly appeared in Beverly's breast a few months after her majestic wedding to Ed. The two of them, both insurance executives, had big plans together. Suddenly breast cancer took over their future and put Beverly on her back. After her mastectomy, she required chemotherapy. I remember visiting her after one of the sessions. She was my first friend to experience cancer. Her hair was gone and her body bone thin. I brought her favorite soup to her, from a cafe nearby but she was too weak to eat. Quietly I was horrified to witness my friend and mentor in such pain and so weak.

•

That was then. This is now. She is a five-year survivor. Her hair is back. She is no longer thin and fragile. She is the strong, beautiful Beverly that I know and love. Surely she could help me. We met for brunch at a chic upscale bistro with a name I could not pronounce. Beverly's words of advice comforted me. She told me that it would be okay. She told me that I would make it through this. I believed her.

Everything was going well over lunch until Beverly handed me the hat. It was a colorful straw hat with a wide brim that she wore when she went through breast cancer. "Here," she said. "You will need this when all of your hair falls out."

But who said I agreed to have cancer anyway?

Beverly was a lot more certain of my situation than I was.

I was still praying that the cancer was a big mistake, and here she was telling me that I'd need her hat to cover up my bald head.

She was smiling. I felt like crap and did not smile. Why should I? I was probably going to die. Big tears streamed down my face. I wanted to go to the restroom and vomit. This had gotten out of hand. Beverly had more than the cancer hat; she also brought a canvas tote with her. It was filled to the rim with breast cancer literature, pins and all types of paraphernalia. Was I going to be struggling with cancer so long that I needed a tote and a hat?

Just a few minutes earlier, I had been comforted by her words of encouragement. But I was unsure now. Despite our friendship and our fashion commonalities, the fear I felt made me resent her. I sat across the table from her over our sophisticated lunch and envied her certainty. She was a bona fide survivor. I was locked in limbo and waiting for results. I was a survivor in waiting. I was a wannabe survivor. I did not know my fate. I wanted Beverly's survivor status. I wanted her happy ending, and that meant cheating the process by skipping the pain and bypassing the suffering to get to the good part.

I drove home from that lunch meeting with my fashion friend wondering, is it my turn to lose hair and not have the strength to eat due to chemotherapy? And was I wrong to want to fast forward through all that hell?

The uncertainties before me could only be balanced out by my must-haves. Those were the things I just could not do without.

CHAPTER 7
Must-Haves

If you are like me, you eagerly await the list of must-have fashion items each season. Whether it is a wide belt, giant bell-bottom slacks or platform shoes, a must-have is just that — something you cannot do without. I have a list of must-haves that enabled me to fight the cancer battle: an armload of fashion magazines, a magnificent hairdresser, a marvelous makeup professional and a supportive spouse.

You must have fashion magazines.

I had armloads of fashion magazines. Sitting curled up with them, I was transported to another place. The traveling was good for me. I could forget about my situation and focus on the beauty. The clothes, the photography, the shoes, the way the pages spoke to me, moved me forward and prevented me from looking back. They pushed me ahead into the next season, and I liked that. They had all the answers to life's most serious problems like... a run in your hose or having muffin top. *If I keep reading, maybe they will have an answer for my problem,* I thought several times. The pages of my mags were dog-eared and smudged because we spent time together. My mags give me some control over my situation. I got to decide if I would embrace the new trend or not.

You must have a magnificent hairdresser.

They say that a hairdresser is part beautician, and part therapist. Mine is all that and more. Tracey has styled my hair for years and over that time, we developed a closeness that rivals many biological sisters. Tracey is temperamental, moody and one of the best hair stylists around. I trust her hair decisions implicitly. She knows and accepts my obsession with what I call "make them holla" hair. If there is no public affirmation to my hairstyle, she has not done her job. My weekly appointments are early in the morning, so no one intervenes on my time to pour out my deepest fears. Those appointments are more than hair styling. They are bonding and caring and sharing times.

The sharing continued after my diagnosis. Tears sprang to Tracey's eyes when I told her I had breast cancer. She was afraid for me and the tears were an immediate reaction to the fear that my cancer could be terminal. Her salon gave me the place where I could speak my mind freely without judgment. I could let it all hang out with her. She was not a cancer survivor, but she empathized with my struggles. Between the shampoo, conditioner, blow dry and flat iron, something cathartic happened for me.

Tracey promised me that I would look good through all of this. If I was going to lose my hair due to chemotherapy, she had a wig already picked out. If my hair was dried out and fragile due to radiation, she had a fab hair cut to suggest. She did not fail. My hair looked marvelous the entire time.

•

You must have a marvelous makeup professional.

A strong relationship with a makeup professional is a must. The world of makeup can be overwhelming. There is so much of it, and all the ads promise to make us look like super models. Do not fall into the trap of owning the right makeup, but applying it incorrectly.

That is where a trusted makeup professional can help. You must have your makeup professional's number on speed dial on your phone. He or she needs to become your new best friend. Spend time with him or her learning what products work best on your skin, how much product you need and how to apply the product. Once you purchase the product, go home and apply it yourself. Return to him or her the next day and ask — is this right?

Over time, as your relationship develops, he or she should inform you of the new shades for the seasonal changes, and put you on his or her speed dial too.

When you're battling cancer, or any tough time in your life, knowing that you look good — whether it's your clothes, hair or makeup — can make you feel better as you go about your day.

•

Robert, my spouse of 25 years, is also a must-have, in season and out of season. He is my calm and serene banker husband. Breast cancer shook me but not him. He was the calm that balanced my frenetic. He was the quiet that balanced my high volume. We have a history of tackling major events as a team, whether buying a house or deciding on schools for our sons. He knows how to give and take, compromise and communicate.

But I was a realist. A breast cancer diagnosis threw all that history out of the window. I started over. No assumptions. No depending on previous behavior. All bets were off. If I assumed, assumption might set me up for great disappointment.

I heard that breast cancer could destroy marriages. It's strange how that information rose up from my memory. I certainly did not summon it. It made me tremble to know that cancer could rip a husband and wife apart. The treatments, the surgery and the unceasing pain could be lethal to matrimony.

I read up on it and saw numerous spouses who fled once they heard their wives had cancer. One man said, "I can't imagine being in the midst of that."

Another said, "I could not bear to watch her die."

A third said, "If she is going to die, why should I stick around and watch?"

When I received the phone call telling me that there were specks found on my mammogram film, Robert was the first and only person I called. Although it was an automatic response to reach out to him when trouble arose, there was also some apprehension. Part of me did not want to tell him. I was not sure what his reaction would be, and mine already was out of control. I considered not telling him at all. And wondered how long I could keep the dreadful news to myself — days, weeks, months?

Although he never uttered a negative word, I quietly worried. Would he want a wife with cancer in her breast? Would he deem me undesirable? Or would this news be a convenient exit strategy?

But, honestly, fear of marital strife paled in comparison to my fear of sickness and death.

I did not want to surrender my marriage to cancer, so I devised a strategy. I kept Robert closely involved every step of the way. I wanted him in the loop in all my health concerns. It was clear that I was in the driver's seat. I had the right to decide what steps I took. He understood and offered great advice from the passenger side.

His response to the news was, "It's your turn now."

I knew what he meant. It had been barely two years since he faced life-threatening heart valve replacement surgery. He was off his feet for weeks, and I was by his side the whole time. Now, we switched places, and he was glad he was not in the hospital again. He clarified the roles we played. This time, I was the sick one; he was the helper.

I listened to what he told friends and family about my situation. He talked about my cancer as if it were one of his banking deals. He said matter-of-factly: "Sheron has breast cancer. They found it early, and she will be fine."

I believed him when I could not believe myself.

His valiant efforts helped me with the dark days when I felt hopeless and helpless. On those days he let me say what was on my mind without any censoring. I peppered him with questions about death that he couldn't answer, just to determine whether he was still strong. I weighed my husband's possible responses as I ran the gauntlet of treatments and procedures through my mind.

"Am I going to die?"

"No."

"How do you know that I am not going to die?"

"I just know."

"What are you going to do if I die?"

"You are not going to die."

The impact of breast cancer on a couple's sex life is huge. Even though sex was the last thing on my mind, how I would look having sex, as a woman with cancer, did cross my mind. If I did need a mastectomy, sex with only one breast could have been my future. I wondered if it would matter to him. Would he still want me minus a breast? What if I went through radiation and my skin became rubbery? There were lots of unanswered questions about intimacy, whether I had time to think about them or not. I contemplated my new appearance in the boudoir. How would I look in lingerie after a mastectomy? How much lace and frill would be required to cover up the missing breast? Where do you purchase items like that? And most importantly — were the items going to be cute?

Even though I did not want sex, I did want intimacy. Hugs, embraces and kisses were enough to keep me going on the breast cancer journey that I still was not sure I was going to participate in. Sex stayed on the back burner as I dealt with a strong emotion — anger.

CHAPTER 8

A Wrap Dress
Called Anger

*A*nger began to swath me with an all-embracing feel, just like a wrap dress. And before I knew it, I was all wrapped up in it.

I am partial to wrap dresses. They swath me in fabric and it feels good. They are the most timeless and kindest dress style in a woman's wardrobe.

Waist-whittling, bust-enhancing and hip-reducing, women of all sizes and ages adore them. The wrap dress was created in the early 1970s by fashion designer Diane Von Furstenberg. The dress has had such an influence on fashion that it is currently on display at the Metropolitan Museum of Art.

Anger came upon me gradually, unexpectedly and strong. Anger is the second stage of grief. Mine felt aggressive and honestly, it felt good to release such raw emotions. Some Christians shy away from anger because they consider it negative, but Jesus got angry about negative situations in his world.

John 2:15 tell us that he was so angry that He turned over the table of the merchants who used the temple as a bazaar. He made a whip out of cord and drove them out.

So certainly I too could get angry. My negative situation was the breast cancer, and it was about to intensify.

Anger arrived during a phone call from my breast cancer doctor's office. A nurse called to give me the results of the lumpectomy. I expected good news. After all, the cancer was located in a small area that could be removed.

Nurse: "Hello, Sheron, this is Janet from the doctor's office. I have some not so great news for you."

Me: "OK." *What is it?*

Nurse: "The results of the lumpectomy came back. We were not able to get all the cancer out. We are going to have to remove the entire breast."

Me: "Say what?"

Nurse: "The cancer has spread all over the breast. We are going to need to remove it."

Me: "There has got to be another way to handle this. Can you remove a larger section and leave some of the breast intact?"

Nurse: "No, that is not possible."

Me: "Well, why isn't it possible?"

Nurse: "This is the only way."

Me: "Well, we need to find another one fast."

Quickly I lunged into a battle over my breast. I was like a wild animal protecting her young. My breast was at stake and I did not plan on surrendering it without a struggle. The nurse and I argued back and forth. She was relentless and so was I.

Perhaps she made lots of calls to women about losing their breasts. This was my first, and I was not taking it well at all. Eventually I gave in because it was pointless to continue. "Okay," I finally told her. "Fine."

I felt anger rising up.

I blamed God for it all. God has all power. The power sure was not working on my behalf. *What happened to all those prayers and all that fasting I did a few weeks ago?* I wondered. As I replayed the conversation in my head, I could not find any reason to continue to hold on to this thing called faith. *God could have stepped in and changed everything around to my favor. It looked like God just sat back and allowed hell to break loose in my life.* Resentment filled my heart. *Thank you, God.*

I refused to pray.

I wanted to take a page from Job's wife who told him to "curse God and die." That did not sound too bad at the moment. I needed to blame someone. Cancer was not what I planned for my life.

I tried to make sense of the cancer diagnosis. *I am a believer. I am faithful. I am a pastor.* I checked off all the things on the list that made me good or "worthy" of being spared this disease. *Why is cancer in my body? I am doing all the right things — healthwise. I drink plenty of water, eat lots of vegetables and fruit, exercise at least five days a week and keep stress to a minimum. And there is no history of breast cancer in my family.*

The biggest question of all kept bouncing around my head: *Why me?*

From anger, I rode the express bus to depression. I rehearsed the worst possible outcomes. I told myself: "You will be a woman with a missing breast. You will not be happy. You will be disfigured and life will be wretched forever."

This negative mantra danced around in my head. I was defenseless against it. Pretty soon, a full-scale pity party was in progress. I was a puppet of despair. My world went gray, even though God sent the sunshine every day.

I could not eat or sleep.

I was numb.

Shame covered me.

Embarrassment took hold of me, and the doctor had not started to cut yet. The reality of physical disfigurement was in my face.

Yes, I was depressed, but I was a functionally depressed person. I kept up my daily routine. I went to work as the senior pastor of a church; I took care of the family and pretended that nothing was wrong. The only thing worse than being disfigured was having everyone know that you are upset about being disfigured. Keeping up my façade of being okay helped me juggle the two Sherons, one hurting, and one happy.

Who could relinquish a trusted body part and friend without a proper goodbye? My breasts had been with me since birth. From the days of the pre-teen training bra, to the current 34 B cups, they were a vital part of me. They filled out my sweaters and T-shirts just right. They gave my physique its snap, crackle and pop.

How could I dismiss one of them now, without fanfare?

The sorrow of mourning for my breast became a constant thought. There was no date set yet for the mastectomy. My doctor told me that there was no rush because the cancer was not aggressive, and had not spread. Since I had the luxury of extra time to mourn my fate I began the process of saying goodbye to my left breast. This was an odd exercise to say the least, but it helped me face my fear, come out of denial and help myself. This was a time of authentic goodbye. I wrote a poem.

Goodbye Poem

Goodbye old friend
I've known you since way back when
I guess this is the end
Who knows if I will see you again?

Deep into my depression, the Lord came and found me. God poured out revelation to lift me up and remind me that loss was not automatically a bad thing when you walk in faith. Jesus experienced loss, but he did not throw in the towel or give up. He pressed through the loss and found gain. Concerning loss, Jesus tells us in **Matthew 16: 25** (The Message Bible), **"Self-sacrifice is the way, my way, to finding yourself, your true self. What kind of deal is it to get everything you want but lose yourself? What could you ever trade your soul for?"**

My bad news was God's good news, in disguise. God does something great with what appears to be our losses. They are not times of loss, but they are times of gain.

Allow me to give the Sheron remix of the version I just quoted: "She who wishes to save her breast, shall lose it, and whoever loses it and keeps the faith shall find something greater."

I was ready to move beyond the pity party. I realized that you can do everything right and still cancer will come. Sometimes, despite your best efforts, trouble comes. Sometimes after you've done your best, situations fall apart. Sometimes, even though you had good intentions, stuff hits the fan, and there is nothing that you can do to prevent it.

I felt Christ with me in this struggle, and knew that in his name, the loss would not end up horribly. In a strangely beautiful way, I felt victorious about the whole mastectomy situation. I felt like I would lose my breast, but gain something better.

God turned this midnight into midday.

God had not failed me yet. There was a shift in me. All

of the shopping to bargain with God, the being too angry to pray was over. Now I was back to being one of the best-dressed soldiers on the battlefield for my Lord and I had to make sure that everything matched.

CHAPTER 9

Mix and Match

One of my earliest fashion lessons was that the clothes I wore should match from head to toe. Growing up, there was never a time when I was not totally color coordinated. It just did not happen. I understand that today's fashion dictates are open and easygoing. Designers even encourage non-matchy dressing. They say wear a pink suit with blue shoes, for example. But I was raised on matching and it is hard to shake.

Because of this, I could not fathom a left breast and a right breast that did not match. A left breast that was newly reconstructed and perky and a right breast that was original and slightly sagging would never do. They simply had to match. What a dilemma for me.

I prayed before I made the decision to have both breasts removed with a double mastectomy. **"God, you said, I am fearfully and wonderfully made." Psalm 139: 14.**

I believed that I am fearfully and wonderfully made, and because of that, I wanted to hang on to as much of my fearfully and wonderfully as possible. My reasons for the double mastectomy (bilateral mastectomy) were two-fold. First, my aesthetic concerns were undeniable. Secondly removing both breasts eliminated the dread that cancer would appear in the remaining healthy breast.

I walked into my breast cancer doctor's office on my next visit and said with the conviction of a woman who could see a new pair of breasts in her future: "If you need to take one breast, take them both, and give me a new pair that is better than before."

It felt good to ask for what I wanted, and it felt even better to receive what I asked for. He agreed to my request.

I shared my surgery plans with a handful of friends and family. The double mastectomy puzzled some people; they did not know how to respond. Some thought it was odd to surrender both breasts when only one had cancer. Others just looked at me with a puzzled expression. Others nervously giggled at the thought that they too, could reach beyond what was expected, to what was unexpected. Some blushed, and their body language revealed that they were ill at ease with the topic of new breasts. A small number were energized by the power of choice. I wanted to energize thought. I wanted my health decisions to liberate as many as possible from the boxes that held them captive.

Sharing my decision made me feel as though I was on *Cancer on Center Stage*. This is the place that lots of people with cancer arrive at when others learn of their situations and offer their remarks about their health choices. *Cancer on Center Stage* came with a live studio audience. Their seats were so close to the stage that you could hear all of their remarks from their gasps to their oohs. Although I had an audience, the decision was mine. I owned it. I was not uncertain or wobbly. I was firm and resolute.

The way I saw it, this choice was my way of declaring self-love and self-preservation. Yes, a double mastectomy was major surgery for stage 0 cancer, but for me, it was a zesty and passionate way of responding to impending disaster. I was taking the tragedy and turning it into triumph. The double mastectomy was a gutsy and audacious way to refuse to be silenced or forced to cower. Some people expected me to lower my head and slink off into a corner and whimper. No, I decided to turn a decision into celebration of power of choice.

I stood at the intersection of faith and fashion — again. My faith taught me that I was valued by God. This meant that I should value and treasure myself too. My fashion sense taught me that mismatched breasts would not do.

The road to new breasts was a refreshing detour off the breast cancer road that I had been on. What a contrast. On the one hand, I lost one breast. On the other hand, I gained a brand new set, and the cancer was removed. There are numerous types of breast reconstruction. My doctor and I decided that mine would be a latissimus dorsi muscle flap. In this surgery, a portion of the back muscle known as the latissimus dorsi was removed, threaded through the body and attached to the chest area. This procedure also included tissue expanders. Tissue expanders were like deflated balloons inflated to stretch the skin to the desired size after surgery.

They were temporary. Once the desired size was achieved they were exchanged surgically for implants months later.

I had to quickly digest this high-tech, medical-marvel lingo because things were moving fast. My breast cancer doctor referred me to a plastic surgeon. This was a jolt. The two of them would operate on me together. This was a bittersweet referral. I felt like I was abandoning the doctor who lifted me up with spiritual power when I was at my lowest. I clung to him like ivy on a wall. Now there would be three of us. Was I ready to add someone else to the team? I hesitated to go to the plastic surgeon's office, even though it was in the same medical building as the breast cancer doctor, but on a higher floor. This medical building is adjacent to the hospital where I had the surgery.

I gasped as I walked into the plastic surgeon's ultra modern office. I entered the mecca of bling and was star struck. The waiting room was magnificent. There were marble floors, expensive artwork and exquisite furniture. This place was elegant, upscale and highly charged with beauty and aesthetics. I felt beautiful just sitting there.

The women that I sat among were in the process of beautification. A nose job over there, a tummy tuck and a little lipo in the corner. I joined their beauty quest. Suddenly, I did not feel like a woman battling cancer. I felt like a Hollywood starlet. They have time and money for plastic surgery. So I pretended that I was one of them. I forgot the cancer. This was nice.

The plastic surgeon's staff members were gorgeous. When one of them escorted me to an examining room I could not keep from staring at her head-to-toe beauty. *I want whatever procedure she got,* I said to myself. The examining room had floor to ceiling glass walls. There were sweeping views of the hospital next door. My head swiveled back and forth between the hospital, where I would surrender my breasts, and this room, where my breasts would be redesigned, until I was dizzy. I was dizzy and delighted to be there.

In walked the plastic surgeon. He fit the bill of the ones I'd seen on television reality shows — dashing, suave, chatty. As he examined and measured my breasts, he asked, "What size would you like them to be?"

My face went completely blank. I never had the freedom to determine the size of my breasts. I was stunned and silent. He quickly realized that I was a plastic surgery rookie in need of direction. He handed me a book and calmly said, "Take a look at this. Pick out what you want." Then he left the room for 15 minutes.

Take your pick? Is that what he said to me? I think I will, I said to myself with bubbling euphoria. In my hands was the breast book, a compilation of photos of previous patients. He reconstructed and augmented their breasts. Now it was my turn. Their privacy was not compromised. No faces were shown, only his majestic handiwork.

Take your pick? Is he serious? I felt like a kid in a candy store! My hands tingled as I gingerly gripped the closed book in my hand. I hesitated to open it. I knew that once I looked at the possibilities, I would never be the same. I wanted to savor this segment of my cancer journey, because it was not what I expected the day I dissolved into tears in the office of my breast cancer doctor. I looked around the room and out of that panoramic glass wall and I thanked God for this strange blessing. I truly was blessed.

I took a deep breath and opened the book. Before me were a host of options. Page after page, there they were: large, small, wide and narrow breasts, all admirably done. Midway through the book I found them, a wonderfully sculpted pair of breasts that I believed would look great on me. I looked no further.

When the surgeon returned, I happily pointed to what I wanted. "I'll take these please," I said.

He looked at my selection and smiled. "You have chosen well."

Not only had I chosen well in my new breast selection, but I also chose to reframe my situation. I was aware that God was moving in my life and I prayed like I knew it too.

"God, you said you did not give me a spirit of timidity, but a spirit of power, of love and self-disciple," I prayed, remembering

2 Timothy 2:17. It was time to act like I knew it. I got tired of being afraid. This is called the acceptance stage of grief, and once I got there, I was no longer sad. I saw my chance to use God's power in my situation, and I did. I refused to let cancer take away all my options. Cancer could no longer dominate me. I got my joy back. I found joy in this struggle.

My duo of doctors set a surgery date of May 7. I could not keep my situation to myself. As the elders say, I could not hold my peace. I had a story to tell. The world should know what God was doing in my life.

My husband knew, many of my friends knew, but I had not told my two sons yet.

CHAPTER 10

My Shoes, My Sons, My Secrets

I have a mild shoe addiction and I have lots of shoes: platforms, wedges, stilettos, sneakers, loafers, flats, mules and flip-flops. Some of my shoes are blinged out. The rhinestone boots were too much to pass up. It's not like a drug or alcohol addiction. I can stop any time that I want, but why would I? I am told that the average woman has 19 pairs of shoes at one time, and will have 469 pairs over her lifetime. Let's just say that I have lots of lifetimes in my closet. Shoes are objects of beauty and I store my beauty in boxes stacked high in my closet. Without exception, I cannot walk past the shoe department of a store without stopping. Something beckons me. I cannot resist. It is a magnificent obsession.

I have a shoe secret too. Some of the shoes I own, I will never wear. I get joy from simply owning them. I open their boxes, ogle their beauty, smell the leather, admire the detailed craftsmanship and put the lids back on the boxes. These are my collectors' items. They are like precious stamps to the philatelist. A few moments with them every now and then, and I feel calm, cool and collected. However, my shoe secret pales in comparison to my breast cancer secret I kept from my sons.

Family secrets are rarely good. Most family secrets are bombshells waiting to explode. They promise and deliver shrapnel to maim whoever is in harm's way. My breast cancer diagnosis was a heavy burden on my soul. I kept it a secret from my two sons Robert Jr., a college student, and Christian, a high school student. I did not know how to tell them that I had cancer. Funny how I could talk to practical strangers about my breasts, but I could not tell my sons. Before I told the world, I paused to tell them. I was excited about my testimony publicly, but I worried about my sons privately.

Mothers and sons often have strong bonds, and the three of us do. We spend lots of time together, watching music videos inside and playing basketball outside. During this journey I put up a strong front when they were around. I thought I was a convincing actress. I was certain that they had no idea of my struggles. I did not want them to know, at least not yet. I had to get myself together first. I had to figure everything out before I brought them into my private hell. It is not the child's job to worry along with the parent. I refused to burden them with my problem.

Even though I did not know how to tell them, I refused to let cancer to come between us. Cancer was dividing us because it halved me into the public and private Sherons. My sons knew nothing of the December mammogram that went wrong, or the January biopsy and lumpectomy.

They did not know that I had a breast cancer doctor, or a plastic surgeon.

My May 7 surgery date was now two months away and they had no clue about it. All they knew was that I was their ever-healthy mom. I was the mom who went to the gym every morning, who drank lots of water, and who was a careful eater because she wanted to stay healthy.

They did not know the other Sheron; the one who learned how to cry silently so they would not hear me, the one who laughed and played with them when she'd rather curl up in a ball and try to disappear, and the one who came into their rooms at night and watched them as they slept because she did not know if she would be around later.

I planned to share this news with them in the least harmful way. Was that even possible? What would they think when I told them? Would they become depressed, like I was? Would they see me as a failure at staying healthy? Would their grades drop in school?

I looked for the perfect time. There was no such thing. There was no perfect way to say what I needed to say to them. Both were heading into final exams. Did I risk telling them and possibly cause their grades to falter?

Here is what I did. Chris was sitting in the den. I sat at the kitchen table and arranged breast cancer books around me. He was an avid reader; maybe when he saw the books he would decide to read up on my situation.

"Chris, come in and talk to me for a second," I calmly asked.

"No. I don't want to."

This was an odd response; Chris was usually upbeat and obedient.

"Why not?"

He knew something was up, but how? Obviously, my disguise had failed. He knew that something was wrong by the sound of my voice. I asked again, and reluctantly, my son came to the kitchen. He saw the books and looked puzzled.

"I need to tell you something. Have a seat."

"Okay. What is it?" he said, staring at the books.

"Chris, I have breast cancer. But I am not going to die."

"Mom, please don't die," he pleaded, as tears welled up in his eyes. I wished it were that easy. The doctor told me that my cancer was nonaggressive and surgery would handle it, but when did cancer ever play fair? No, cancer plays dirty. It double-crosses and cheats all the time. Nevertheless, I lied to my youngest son with a straight face.

"I won't die," I said.

I offered him books to read on the topic, answered a few more of his questions with lies and hopes. Then I made a mad dash to the telephone, to call Robby, before Chris could.

"Robby, I've got something to tell you," I announced timidly.

"Go ahead," said a baritone college-man voice on the other end of the phone. He probably thought I wanted to talk about his summer job or some other chore I had for him.

"I have a health challenge."

"What is it?

"I don't want you to be upset."

"So just tell me, "Robby demanded, clearly irritated with my halting delivery.

"I have breast cancer. I am going to have a double mastectomy and reconstruction soon." I blurted it out fast. "Are you all right?"

"Of course I am all right. I am not a child. I can handle stuff like this."

"Robby, it is going to be all right," I said, hoping to convince him.

"Okay, Mom," he replied, voice never wavering.

"I love you. Goodbye."

After I made my cancer revelation, it seemed that my relationship with my sons changed. There was uneasiness between us, thick enough to be cut with a knife. I felt as if they looked at me differently. They were quieter, as if the silence would soothe their wounds. Maybe they thought I was weaker and more fragile. Their rambunctious horseplay around the house stopped when I came around. Even their merciless teasing of me subsided. They treated me differently because I had cancer, and I did not like it. But I did understand it and respected it. In fact, I grew to enjoy my short-lived respite from the rough housing. I took it and gave them the space they needed to process what my cancer meant to them.

Before you read any further, I want to let you know that I had a hard time telling my congregation about my breast cancer, too. I had always been the healthy, exercising pastor who promoted all types of churchwide programs to get them on the health track with me. I preached on the topic, taught on the topic and walked on the topic — literally, leading them in everything from running in marathons to building a community vegetable garden in the back of the church to swing-out dance lessons in the fellowship hall.

The Sunday I stood before them and said that I had cancer was a blow to my pastoral confidence. I was supposed to be the strong one. I was the one who ate fresh fruit and vegetables, and I had cancer? Was God playing a cruel joke? Was God embarrassing me in front of my flock? I felt like a failure.

There was not a dry eye in the sanctuary. After we dried our collective tears, we moved into a new way of relating to each other. The roles were about to reverse. I learned how to accept help and concern, instead of dishing it out. I needed this more than I realized. It was a joy to be prayed for, comforted, hugged and surrounded by a faithful flock. That is what they did, because that is what they are.

•

Now that my husband, my sons and my congregation

knew, I was really ready to tell the world about my blessing and get ready for the surgery. But there was one more move to make first: A trip to North Carolina to tell my parents.

CHAPTER 11

Generational Glamour Girl

If ever there is research conducted on whether glamour is inherited, put my momma and me in the group to be studied. I am certain that my fashion flair comes directly from her. A peek in her closet reveals metallic, rhinestone-encrusted loafers. The bling is in the blood. She is a timeless beauty. Photos of her back in the day depict a young woman with shoulder-length coal black hair in leather coats with fox trim and fitted suits with gloves. In the photos she was always smiling. She was happy to look so good.

My earliest memories growing up are shopping with her in downtown Charlotte, North Carolina. We made a day of it and never got tired. We shopped all morning, paused for lunch, then shopped all afternoon. The remnants of segregation prevented us from shopping in the toniest of stores. Momma felt strongly that the stores that once kept African Americans out were not about to get her money after desegregation. Not to be outdone, she patronized a Jewish-run clothier on a regular basis. Whenever we arrived, my momma's favorite sales clerk greeted us with pre-selected items or outfits my momma requested that the owners purchase for her on their buying trips to New York.

Aging has not changed her much. Mom is 70-ish, never one to reveal the exact age. Her coal black hair tussles with gray strands, but the gray strands lose every week at the hair salon as fresh dye is applied. She still dresses up with the latest jewelry, purses and suits. And I would be remiss if I did not give a fashion nod to my dad. He too is a snazzy dresser. My dad and my mother never leave the house without a tailored, well-coordinated look.

My parents are churchgoing people. Every Sunday morning, and often through the week, we were at church. They were not pew sitters either. Both are leaders and major contributors to the congregation. Their faith became my faith, and it is because of them I have a deep and abiding love for the assembly of believers. And there is a strong connection between dressing up and the African American church. Church, for many, was the only place we had to dress up and put on our Sunday best. Sunday clothes and shoes are traditions from my parents' childhood that they passed down to me.

My dad speaks nostalgically of his childhood Saturday night ritual of preparing his Sunday best. After his Saturday evening bath, he would press and lay out his pants, shirt, tie, socks and shined shoes, in anticipation of going to church on Sunday morning.

So, I got on a plane and flew 1,000 miles to tell them in person that I had breast cancer. I could not tell them over the phone. I thought they would fall apart. The news that their only child had been diagnosed with breast cancer may be too much to handle. I had been turned upside down, wouldn't they be also?

The flight from Dallas to Charlotte was not long enough to figure out my strategy for telling them. I could not determine if I should tell them at the airport, or in the car heading to their home, or over lunch, or as we turned in that night for bed.

At the airport terminal we hugged and embraced. Not yet.

We exchanged pleasantries. *You sure look good. I love those shoes.* Not yet.

Where did you get that purse? It sure is pretty. Not yet.

How are Robert and the boys? Not yet.

I looked at them and could not determine a time to tell my challenging news. My parents were aging. All parents do. They were grayer, slower and even appeared smaller to me. I thought the weight of what I had to say might crush them.

I recalled **Psalm 37:25** and uttered a tiny prayer: "God, your word said, **'I was young and now I am old yet I have never seen the righteous forsaken or their children begging bread'**" Give me the strength to tell them.

•

After a good ole southern lunch of smothered chicken with squash and collard greens from their backyard garden, we sat in the den and basked in being together some more. This was the time.

"Mom, Dad, I have something to tell you."

They kept on smiling. They assumed that I had good news because that's all I ever brought them. Their trusting smiles made me reluctant to proceed with my bitter truth. Perhaps I should have made up something else to tell them. But my faith kicked in and I said exactly what I had flown all those miles to tell them.

"Mom and Dad, I have breast cancer. It has been found in only one breast, but I am having a double mastectomy with reconstruction."

It spilled out of my mouth like water spilled out of a cup that is knocked over. The words splashed out and into the room. I waited for them to fall apart, weep, wail or just look scared. None of that happened.

They kept smiling and said, "Baby it will be fine. Do what you need to do. It will work out."

Without question their fashion sense had guided me through life, but it could never overshadow the power of the Word of God these two churchgoing people also reared me in. They were living proof of the power of the scriptures. The weight of secrets was lifted off me and like an athlete in training I was able to run a lot faster. Now I had even more energy and excitement about what God was doing. I felt like I was launching a new product line — God's new line in my life!

CHAPTER 12

Launching My Line

I launched a motivational/inspirational product line that moved women into breast cancer awareness and away from fear about the dreaded disease. It was my breast cancer project. This launch required the same guts it takes to launch a fashion line. The experts say that launching a fashion line is a matter of risk, research and gut feelings. It is also about style, fabrics, colors and cuts, and what the customers will buy. A buzz is desired, which will translate to the public embracing your garments. The same was true for my program. This thing was irrepressible. I could not keep it to myself.

Of course I am not the prophet Jeremiah, but maybe I know how he felt when he said he could not keep the news about the goodness of God to himself. Jeremiah wrote, **"His word is in my heart like a fire, a fire shut up in my bones. I am weary of holding it in." Jeremiah 20:9.**

God moved in a mighty way in my life. He brought me from cancer diagnosis to the brink of brand-new breasts! I was about to burst open. Who could keep that news inside? I was not gloating. I was grateful.

I had to tell the world what God was doing in my life. I let people know that I was in the midst of this cancer fight, and let them know that God was my power and my strength. Going public meant telling everybody I knew, through every media channel possible. There was no shame, embarrassment or fear this time. I was jubilant.

I felt a strong urge to be somebody else's blessing. I had been rescued for a reason. I dared not ask why. The appropriate response was to run and help someone. Unto whom much is given, much is expected. The best way for me to help others was sharing my breast cancer journey. My goal was to demystify breast cancer for the general public, encourage women to take care of themselves, and get their annual mammograms.

A friend pulled me to the side and said, "Why do you want to do this? It is nobody's business what you are dealing with."

That was not how I saw it. God placed this situation on

me to help others make it through. My breast cancer doctor was correct. He spoke prophetically into my life and now my actions illustrated his words. Not only would I tell the world, but I wanted to empower the world to live healthy. It was, after all, a routine mammogram that caught the cancer in its earliest stage and thereby saved me. I promoted mammograms as a key to health. Early detection saves lives.

The perfect venue to launch my breast cancer project was a women's health event at a local hospital. I was the keynote speaker. The title of my address was "Show Yourself Some Love." It was a dress-up affair. The women looked marvelous, and so did I. I wore a peach-colored dress with a double strand turquoise necklace, with matching bracelet and earrings.

I told them, "Take care of your bodies because they are temples of the Holy Ghost. You have the Holy Ghost in you. Do you realize that?

"We women have a habit of putting ourselves last. We take care of the cat and the dog and the neighbors down the street. But who takes care of us?"

The audience was with me. Their body language said, *"Yes, we hear you."* The atmosphere was filled with positive energy. They sat on the edges of their seats. Some even clapped and cheered. Then I shared my health situation.

"My temple is under attack right now from cancer, but I believe God that it will be all right."

The room went silent. The women who had been smiling and absorbed in the encouragement stopped smiling. They did not know how to absorb this. Some looked baffled. Others had worry and concern etched on their faces. I threw them a curve. A curve had been thrown at me. I handled mine. They could handle it too. I was there to champion health and wellness, and suddenly I was telling them that I had cancer. They did not know whether to cry, laugh, applaud or all of the three.

"In this very hospital, just a few months ago I came in for an annual mammogram and they found cancer. My surgery is set for May 7. I will have a double mastectomy."

This was the ultimate teaching moment because some

women think they could never get a cancer diagnosis.

I made the women in the room think about their health situations because I made them think about mine. It was an aggressive move, but it felt right. I was a living, breathing example of health and sickness. Maybe they would see me as their health role model. I was walking down the road called don't be afraid, just deal with whatever health concerns come along. I was at peace with the matter because it was presented in a manner that lifted up women and made them think about themselves as they thought about me. Maybe I stunned them. Maybe I scared them, but this plan worked. How did I know? Afterward many women hugged me, prayed for me and wanted to stay in touch. They were ready to go where God and I were taking them. They got onboard with my health journey, not realizing that they started their own.

Members of the media were there too. Thanks to them, news of my breast cancer diagnosis was broadcast all over the city. A radio station broadcast from the luncheon and interviewed me live. They wanted to have the scoop on this. Maybe they thought I was going to die. Maybe I was, but on the way to the grave I was going to help as many people as I could — while looking good.

Something God happened when I gave of myself and decided to go public. God poured back into my life. "God, you said, **'Test me in this says the Lord Almighty, and see if I will not throw open the floodgates of heaven for you and pour out such a blessing that you will not have room enough for it.'"** **Malachi 3:10**

God poured and poured. More media joined me. Maybe they looked for a sensational story; but in reality they spread the good news of God and the testimony of a grateful woman.

"Local pastor goes public with cancer fight," was the lead story on television stations.

Newspaper headlines blared the same. Both mediums decided to follow my journey — all the way to surgery and beyond. All of this gave God glory and told the world that silence was not what God wanted from us.

God was not done. His most amazing act was connecting me with a hospital to create a woman's health empowerment program. I wanted to reach hundreds of women with my story in order to motivate them toward healthy living. With the hospital's health program, the media's reach and my faith, we formed a citywide movement toward women's health empowerment called "The Patterson Pledge." The four-part health promise helped women live a healthy lifestyle. They pledged: I will get a mammogram annually. I will exercise regularly. I will eat healthy food regularly. I will stop the stinking thinking.

The pledge program provided refrigerator magnets, lapel pins, a health diary and podcasts that were all tailored to help women to take charge of their health.

I was a catalyst. I changed how women viewed their health. I made the right decision to go public. My health struggle was not meant to be fought quietly behind the scenes. No. God wanted everyone to watch God's glory. Finally I had confidence that God would see me through, and I wanted others to feel the same way about God. I wanted others to join me on the journey, whether they had cancer or not. God was taking me somewhere great, and I was not going alone. I was taking as many as I could with me to witness the power of the Lord.

May 7 quickly approached. I had custom-made hope in mind to carry me further along on the journey.

CHAPTER 13

Hope Couture

Couture means custom made. Haute couture is the height of custom-made clothing. It is French for high sewing or high dressmaking. It refers to garments made of high quality fabrics that are created with great detail. Only a gifted seamstress can create such. I own only a few haute couture garments, but what I needed right now was a spiritual garment of hope couture for my surgery. My hope is a product of my faith. To get my faith going I prayed, "God, you said, my faith is being sure of what I hope for and certain of what I do not see."

I celebrated my birthday on May 6. It was a blessing to surround myself with people who cared. It was real audacity to celebrate life, when the threat of cancer and death lurked nearby. Finally, May 7 arrived. The weather was beautiful and I felt beautiful even though I knew there was cancer inside me.

I had an eight-hour surgery ahead of me, and I was ready to get it on. I dressed simply for this: a non-embellished jogging suit and plain sneakers. I left all the external bling at home. It was not needed. I was blinging with hope on the inside.

Robert drove me to the hospital in the chilly dawn darkness. We didn't talk much. There was not much to say, except — let's do this. A few prayer warriors had arrived at the hospital. They prayed over me one last time. I appreciated their early morning dedication, but I was eager to move on to the surgery room. I was ready to have this cancer removed from my body, so I could get on with the rest of my life.

I donned a surgical gown with matching hat and socks. They were all the same color. I was still matching. Robert was there to hold my hand. My breast cancer doctor came by to explain everything to me. He made jokes to keep me calm. My plastic surgeon came by too. With cold, felt tipped markers, they sketched out how they would slice and dice my chest. This would have been wildly inappropriate in another setting, but here, I was glad they mapped out their work in advance. There was no time for errors.

A television anchor and his camera crew arrived to tape

another segment of my cancer journey. I insisted that we include my pre-surgery look. Why? I wanted women to see that surgery is not that bad, and that they would be okay if they ever faced cancer. My pride was pushed to the side, as I was videoed sans makeup and jazzy hairstyle. I wanted the viewers to watch this and think, "Wow, she is tackling her cancer problem head-on. I can do the same thing."

We had a festive time and the camera captured it all. I laughed. I smiled. I offered sage advice about the surgery that was about to start. I practiced being calm and collected. I practiced being relaxed and at ease. This came from the realization that firstly, God had it under control and secondly, worry would not change a thing.

It was all about my attitude. Medical science proved that patients with positive attitudes had better surgical outcomes. Finally the party in the surgical preparation room was over. The video crew returned to the news station. The prayer warriors headed home and Robert gave me a goodbye kiss on the forehead. I was wheeled into the surgery room on a gurney, and much to my surprise, there was a party going on there too. I like parties, so I felt right at home. Loud music rocked out of speakers, nurses and attendants scurried around in rhythm as they prepared the room for the removal of my breasts and the cancer that was in one of them. I liked loud music, and people who know how to sway to the beat.

A needle was inserted into my vein, and the next thing I heard was the beeping and clicking of medical machinery. The sounds gently awakened me. The surgery was over and I was in my hospital room. Yes. I was alive. I made it. Thank you, God!

My breast cancer doctor, my plastic surgeon and God were a fierce team. The medical doctors performed the external work and God did the spiritual work.

The room was dark, but I could make out the images of floral arrangements positioned across the room. Nurses buzzed in and out of the room like honeybees, with medicine, bandages, and medical charts. I decided to remain quiet and linger deep inside my thoughts to determine my next move.

I'd love to leap out of the bed and dance in frenzied joy. But my legs said, not now.

My brain reminded me that I had just come from surgery and sent a signal to my hands to check and see if my breasts were there. Who knew? Maybe the doctor duo devised a new plan as I slept. My hands could not reach. The IVs that were taped to both my arms restricted any movement. I lifted my neck to tilt my head downward. I looked down into the opening of my surgical gown and peered at my chest. It was flat and covered in bandages. I was breast-less. They were gone. Strangely, I was okay with this. Did I miss them? Yes, but they were collateral damage in my war against cancer. Nurses came by to examine my former breasts, which they now called my wounds. They were concerned that infection may set in. A mild sting emerged from the bandages.

Yet another stronger source of major pain grabbed my attention. I was stunned to realize that six drains were beside me in the bed and they were attached to my body. They resembled clear plastic grenades strapped to my waist. What a sight in these terror alert days of ours. I read about drains, but nothing prepared me for the experience of having them dangle from my sides. They were gross, but necessary. They allowed blood and bodily fluids to empty from my surgical wounds. Nurses came by around the clock to empty them. The six drains competed with the discomfort and pain from the wounds to win the agony prize. I put them all in check with a double squeeze of the morphine pump.

Despite that pain, I was at peace in the hospital room, with IVs, drains and wounds. My peace was not something that I practiced. It was a gift from the Lord. Jesus delivered it to me, just like the florist delivered the beautiful flowers to my room. I decided whether to accept the gift or not. The alternative was to try to get through that experience on my own. His peace kept me. I was being kept from the pangs of despair. Without peace, I'd feel sorry for myself, wonder about my future and convince myself that something was going to go wrong.

"God, you said, **'Peace I leave with you; my peace I give you.**

I do not give to you as the world does. Do not let your hearts be troubled and do not be afraid.' I need that peace," I prayed, recalling the words of **John 14:27**.

This peace of Jesus was a gift to my soul. It brought tranquility to my heart and clarity to my mind. There was a presence in this present. I knew that I was not alone.

Jesus' peace floated down on me like fresh morning dew and I relaxed in the hospital bed. I took a deep breath to smell the fragrance of my flowers and then snuggled down under the covers to let the medicine flow through my veins. I let the doctor who never lost a patient, work it out.

However, waiting on me was pain so intense, that I needed my faith even more.

CHAPTER 14

Agony Was the Accessory

y closet is brimming with accessories because they complete my outfits. I am partial to chunky bangles, earrings with swing and necklaces that make statements. My accessories have punch and power because they direct my look toward office, casual or after-five. On this breast cancer journey agony became an accessory. Pain from the surgery rose to the level of agony and stayed awhile. In only a way God could design, agony accessorized my newest outfit — outreach.

Before I left the hospital, my doctor duo team came by my room to check on me. I would see my plastic surgeon on a weekly basis soon. I liked the glamorous mood he put me in. My breast cancer doctor told me the lab reports determined that there was no cancer in the right breast, which had been removed along with the left. I remained pleased with my decision for a double mastectomy. Now was no time to waver. I asked if all the cancer was gone. He said he thought it was. I wanted more certainty in his answer, but that was the nature of cancer. Nothing was certain.

Where was my morphine pump? I missed the morphine pump because the pain went home with me. I went home to recover, after spending two days in the hospital. My mother arrived from Charlotte, North Carolina to nurse me back to health.

She effortlessly shifted into the doting mother mode from my childhood. She answered the phone, accepted floral deliveries and kept the house spotless, all the while keeping an eye on her stories or soap operas. Delicious meals streamed out of my kitchen, as if it were a soul food restaurant. Grits, turkey bacon, wheat toast and fruit was breakfast. A tossed salad with grilled chicken was lunch. And baked catfish, floating on a bed of rice and black-eyed peas with cornbread was my dinner. The only trouble was, I was in too much pain to eat.

Also assisting my mom was my 70 lb chocolate Labrador retriever, Lillie. Usually she pounced on me with unbridled canine excitement, but even she knew that I was in extreme pain. Now she quietly lay beside my bed and kept an eye on me day and night. I talked to her and she seemed to understand everything I said. Dogs are amazing in the healing process. Without lifting a paw, they make you feel so much better.

The pain I experienced was intense and unrelenting. The drains tugged and pulled on the small slits in my flesh. With the slightest movement, even breathing, all six of them jostled and sloshed with liquid from my innards. Each contained varied amounts of brownish fluid that trickled from inside me. Walking to the bathroom with them in tow required premeditated planning. Emptying the drains was a task I did not wish on my worst enemy. My mother did it without any complaint.

After two weeks the drains were removed. I would have celebrated but another source of pain immediately took their place like a pair of tag team wrestlers. Now it felt like an Anaconda had taken up residence in my chest. Anacondas are South American snakes that crush their prey by constricting them to death. I was being constricted mercilessly. It tightened and loosened at its will.

Mornings were the worst. No, nights were the worst. I could not breathe, walk or talk during the day or the night. It hurt so badly. If I could, I would have tossed and turned in my bed, but the pain forced me to lie motionless and stiff in the middle of the bed. Sleeping pills and pain pills were my only refuge. No one told me about this relentless pain. It was not mentioned in the breast cancer books that I read. Eventually I learned that the pain was a part of the healing process of the latissimus dorsi or back muscle. A portion of the muscle was cut and stretched around to the front of my chest to replace the cancerous breast muscle that was removed.

Actually my pain had two sources. In addition to the back muscles that now stretched to the front, I had tissue expanders in my chest. My plastic surgeon implanted them during the double-mastectomy surgery. Weeks from now, he would gradually inflate them and they would stretch my skin in preparation for breast implants. Now they were deflated balls beneath the surface. And they throbbed.

I refused to allow the suffering to slow me down or block where God was taking me. I decided that this affliction was a transitional vehicle to my ultimate destination. This understanding took my mind off the bandages that were changed twice daily and my inability to breathe most of the time.

I heard that through sufferings and trials God shaped us into the people God wanted us to be. Something God-like was happening to me again. While I was healing at home I felt strong instead of fragile. I felt concern for others instead of worry about myself. Perhaps I was experiencing something close to what Paul wrote about concerning the pain in his flesh in 2 Corinthians 12:7-10. I began to meditate on this passage. It applied so literally to my life then and there.

"To keep me from becoming conceited because of these surpassingly great revelations, there was given me a thorn in my flesh, a messenger of Satan, to torment me. Three times I pleaded with the Lord to take it away from me. But he said, My grace is sufficient for you, for my power is made perfect in weakness. Therefore I will boast all the more gladly about my weakness, so that Christ's power may rest on me. That is why, for Christ's sake, I delight in weakness, in insults, in hardships, in persecutions, in difficulties. For when I am weak, then I am strong."

I knew what Paul meant when he said that pain brought him back to humility. I had been lifted up and saluted during the launching of the women's health empowerment program, "The Patterson Pledge," but it was really about God. Maybe this was my time to be brought low, and it was not such a bad thing. Being low kept me in touch with the "least of these," specifically, those who had no access to health care. The life-saving mammograms that I readily promoted to any and all who would listen were financially out of reach for a growing population of unemployed or under employed women. The question came to me: What can I do for those without money for mammograms?

The agony would not relent, and I continued to meditate of this Word. In my weakness Christ's power came and rested on me. At my lowest, came a divine directive: *Do more to help women.* My flesh wanted to ignore the directive and focus on the present pain. The directive did not budge. It refused to be pushed aside. Instead it grew larger and detailed. "Why not create projects that express the survivor's gratitude to God for life? From this directive, the gratitude projects — Breast Cancer Builds and Mammograms for the Masses — were born.

I continued to meditate on the scripture as the idea took more form. The words, *my grace is sufficient for you,* flashed through my mind and the thought rose up that God's grace gave us the ability to be brave. My flow of logic said, one must be brave in order to get well. The words brave and wellness came together in my mind and Brave Wellness became the name of the nonprofit organization that would be formed.

How could I start a nonprofit organization from the bed while healing from major surgery? I could not do anything, but God could. My friend Rebel Calhoun came to the rescue. I am giving you her whole name to paint a picture of who she is. Her name is an appropriate moniker. Rebel is a free-spirited woman. She never had cancer, but was excited about Brave Wellness and helped to bring it to life. I was supposed to be in bed in order to heal, but Rebel and I found ourselves around my kitchen table completing nonprofit applications. I was not supposed to leave the house except for doctor's visits, but Rebel drove me to meetings with organizations that breathed life and finances into my projects. I was supposed to be in pain. I praised God for my productive pain. The agony completed my new outfit — outreach. It also prepared me to deal with inner affliction — guilt.

CHAPTER 15

Guilt Is Gaudy

Gaudy is not a word I would use to describe myself or my wardrobe. At least not right now. There have been those occasional lapses into tasteless and flashy, like the time I could not resist the hot pink suede boots with fringe or the neon orange fake fur hat. Actually gaudy fashion is in the eye of the beholder. One woman's trashy is another woman's très chic. The guilt I began to experience about surviving breast cancer was undeniably gaudy. It was completely out of place and unnecessary. But first I had to recognize how wrong I appeared.

The more I recovered, the guiltier I felt. The reality that I survived breast cancer made me second-guess God's plans. I asked questions like: "Why am I still here? Why didn't others survive? "

My wounds soon healed and I was on my way to a new set of breasts. But I could not be satisfied with what God had done. I pestered God with why. Why was I dealt this hand and not them?

There have been others who attempted to question God's plans. Job was one of them. God responded in **Job 38:4: "Where were you when I laid the earth's foundation? Tell me, if you understand. Who marked off its dimensions? Surely you know!"**

Like Job, I knew better, but I could not help but ask. I was embarrassed that the question of "Why me?" refused to leave my mind. I tried to submerge it into the deep recesses of my thoughts, but it tenaciously fought its way to the surface, like one of the unsinkable pool floats. I tried to run from it, but it chased me down like a bloodhound.

Please do not dismiss me as ungrateful to be alive. I was happy each morning that I woke up.

Do not castigate me as a heathen, unable to realize that God blessed my life. Some would say that because I was a pastor, I should not have had these thoughts. But I did. I survived breast cancer (so far), yet millions have not. I thought about those who did not survive, and I questioned, "Why am I still here?"

According to my research, this is called survivor guilt,

a condition in which a survivor of something terrible feels that he or she has somehow done something wrong in making it through the same thing that some others have not survived. Survivor guilt was first noticed in the survivors of the Holocaust, who were plagued by thoughts of why they escaped the horrors of the Nazis, while family and friends did not.

Survivor guilt is experienced by those who have endured combat, natural disasters, automobile accidents and plane crashes. Recent layoffs have created another pervasive category of survivor guilt experienced by those persons who still have jobs, while co-workers were released. In one article I read on this topic, a still employed worker asked, "How do I start up conversations with my former colleagues who are jobless and I still have a paycheck?" She felt guilty because she had a job.

I knew what she meant. Cancer killed women who were close to me, and I felt ashamed to be alive, as if I did something wrong. Their deaths rocked my world. I did not want to lose them. I wondered why cancer claimed them and not me. I also wondered if they had the same thoughts. I was no more deserving of life than they were.

A portion of my survivor guilt was the feeling of inadequacy when newly diagnosed women sought me for counsel. They seemed to flock to me, because I had survived. There were requests from women that I had never met on my voicemail. They had just been diagnosed with breast cancer and they called me because they believed I could help them. They wanted to talk, share their fears and just be heard by the universe. Maybe, just maybe, by talking to me, they gained a glimmer of hope. They hoped I could ensure my fate for them. Yes, I survived, but I did not have the secret password for long life to pass on to others. I wish I had it, then we could form a survivor's sorority and everyone would live.

One woman called because her mother had been diagnosed with Stage IV cancer. Another one emailed that she had just learned that she had the most aggressive form of breast cancer known as Triple Negative. Still a third woman left a message that she needed help telling her husband that she was getting a mastectomy. I had never met these women. They did not know me — personally. They all knew that I was not a doctor. They called because they knew that I did know the ultimate doctor, the one that has never lost a patient. The one that sits high and looks low! That is why they called. It was not even about me. It was about Jesus. So I got myself out of the way and let his power shine through.

The guilt was in check for a while. Then Karen died. My guilt trigger was deaths of friends from cancer. Serving as a pastor to Karen, a woman in the last stages of breast cancer, challenged me. When I first met Karen, my cancer had been detected, treated and I was on the mend, but she was in the midst of a multi-year fight, and was losing. My cancer looked like a walk in the park, while hers raged like an out-of-control forest fire. Cancer first invaded her life when she was a beautiful and vibrant woman. I did not know her then, but photos on her walls presented a gorgeous, fashionable chick that had a lot of life and had a lot of fun.

The woman I visited with communion every month was a fraction of the one on the walls. Slowly cancer forced her from her work, shriveled her body, and stole her hair. Cancer did not cripple her spirit. She was full of spunk and humor when our lives intersected. I visited with her, and prayed with her regularly.

Even when the doctors said there was nothing more they could do, I kept on visiting and praying. As I sat and held her withered, worn hand, I felt guilty. I wondered the entire time if she knew how I felt. I was there to serve as her pastor, but I felt like a fraud.

I wondered when she looked into my eyes, if she was angry that our cancers were so different.

There were laughable times with Karen too. I can never forget the day I walked into her apartment after the plastic surgeon had completed all the chest extender treatments. My breasts had been augmented to match the ones I picked out of the breast book months ago. I had quite a different appearance than before. I felt like a child who had a new bike. Karen looked at me, grinned but did not mention them. I spent an hour there in prayer and Bible study with her and finally she said with a chuckle, "Well did you get them big enough?"

Eventually, Karen died, after her ten-year battle. Preaching her funeral was one of the hardest things I've ever had to do. It was also one of the most empowering. The church was packed and the spirit was high. My musicians were at their best and they hit every note with harmonious zeal. The choir sang like Jesus was about to walk into the sanctuary. This was the perfect home-going for Karen, who once sang in the choir. A parade of people made their way to the pulpit to offer testimonies. Finally it was time for the Words of Remembrance. It was time for the one who survived cancer to preach for the one who did not. I sat in the pulpit, and guilt crept back in as thoughts poured through my head. *Why was my cancer stage 0? Why did it only invade one breast and not the lymph nodes? Why did I get to skip chemotherapy and radiation?*

I stood before the congregation reluctantly. I wanted to say, "Saints, I really should not be here, but I am."

The congregation saw my struggle. They covered me with a shower of "Amen" and "Thank you, Jesus" shouts from the pews. They met every statement I made with affirmation. God spoke through me with great gusto because I could not speak for myself. I told them, "God's grace and mercy has me standing here today and there is a word from the Lord coming from 2 Timothy 4:7. It reads: **'I have fought the good fight, I have finished the race, I have kept the faith. Now there is in store for me the crown of righteousness... .'**"

"When a Fighter Goes Home" was the title of my message.

Karen did not leave this world whimpering or cowering.
Amen.
She left brave and strong.
Thank you, Jesus.
She showed us all that cancer is not the end; it was merely the door out.

Yes.

She maintained her dignity and beauty every step of the way.

Yes.

That is how she let cancer know that she was not giving in or up.

Tell it.

She fought all the way.

Well...

She ran the race.

Well...

Now she has a crown.

Thank you.

Cancer did not win.

Thank you.

God did.

Yes, Lord.

Preaching that sermon gave me a sense of gratitude for not only Karen's life but for the power that God gives us all to handle whatever comes our way. My gratitude grew and it eventually overtook the guilt. I focused in on my purpose for being here. It was not about me, so the guilt was just getting in the way of giving God the glory! I traded my guilt in for gratitude! The guilt was a trap to keep me sad about my blessing. I was blessed and I used my blessing to be a blessing. By exploring my feelings I had a better handle on my emotions. It is always best to confront what we feel. Denial and running away solve nothing.

Now that guilt was under control, there was still another internal matter that needed to be addressed — a spirit of unforgiveness.

CHAPTER 16

A Fashion Don't

What were you thinking when you put that on? Fashion don'ts include panty lines that show through pants, overdoing the animal print in an outfit and wearing black lip liner. They are faux pas and blunders in our attempt to look good. Confession time: I have committed my share of fashion don'ts. I occasionally have panty lines. And I have worn too much animal print at one time. I have used my eyeliner to line my lips. Unforgiveness may not be a fashion don't, but it is one of life's don'ts. I committed this don't as well. Thankfully though, with time, I was able to get rid of this don't.

Have you ever had the feeling that something was missing? That's where I was. The cancer was behind me. I should have had it all together, but I felt like something was missing. I had to reach inside and forgive. Something deep inside told me that there was more to be done. I was blessed with a top-notch medical team, but they could not do it all. I did not expect them to. I had to do some internal work that even the surgeons could not.

I was in the midst of the weekly expander process. Remember those deflated basketballs the doctors placed in my chest during the mastectomy? Over an eight-week period my plastic surgeon and his team injected the expanders with a liquid to increase their size. It was a painful process. My flesh and tissues expanded. Even though it hurt, I did not mind this pain. My breasts were slowly growing larger each week. It was quite a marvel to behold.

The missing feeling sent me on a journey into my spiritual self. I had given my physical body all it needed. Now I needed to focus in on the inner person. This was hard work, but total healing could not come until I rectified this error.

Going internal was prompted by the question of why? Why did I get breast cancer? Where did it come from? Was it my diet? Was it hereditary? As I searched for answers, my neglected spirit finally received the attention that it needed. Sure I prayed and fasted during this ordeal, but my soul needed more attention. It was a nagging need.

I read an article that said breast cancer could be caused

by stressful, anger-filled situations. Anger acts as an internal toxin. I thought about how I handled anger and how anger handled me. I wondered about myself and anger. I decided to include some non-traditional forms of medicine in my search. Lots of cancer patients explore non-Western remedies. My search was not for a cancer cure. I believed that had been handled. I looked for a soul cure.

If you find yourself struggling with unresolved feelings — whether guilt, unforgiveness or some other negative emotion— do not be embarrassed to seek professional help. Your relatives and girlfriends mean well, but get a paid professional to assist you. Stretch outside what you know or what you think you know. Quit being scared to try new things—this is the fight of your life!

I located a Christian who practiced traditional Chinese medicine. She was young, attractive, active in her church and very interested in my breast cancer journey. She also was a sharp dresser and wore the cutest ballerina flats the first day I met her. I relaxed because I believed she could help me go within and deal with my soul, and maybe have a conversation about where she got those shoes.

On our first visit she led me to a small room and had me lay on an examining table — just like in the regular doctor's office. This did not seem weird, just different. She said, "I am going to examine your meridians first." I did not know that I had them and quickly tried to figure out what part of my body she intended to examine.

"Meridians," she explained, "are the pathways through which the body's bio-energy flows." She taped several sensors to pulse points on my body such as my wrist and my ankles, and in a few minutes the results revealed that I had blockages in my meridians. This meant that my energy was not flowing properly. She talked with me more, exploring my eating habits, my sleeping patterns and other windows to my soul. She concluded that the probable issue was unresolved anger in my spirit.

Anger in my spirit! How could meridians pick that up? She was right. I could not admit it to myself. I needed an outside opinion to tell me what I already knew. The missing link in my healing process was my decision not to forgive a past offense.

My spirit was wounded. A very hostile church situation from my past had injured me deeply. A spirit of offense set in and festered. Some people think that pastors are flawless and live perfect lives, but we do not. We are quite human and live under a microscope with inflated, unrealistic expectations.

Everyone gets emotionally hurt in life. Some refuse to release the hurt, and the wounds cripple them. I have always been one to bounce back from hurt feelings, but I encountered an experience that was toxic. None of my advanced degrees prepared me for the deep gash that was left behind. I internalized the pain and never let it escape. The unresolved anger led to unforgiveness inside me. Although no doctor confirmed this, I believed this could be the cause of the cancer.

There is a twisted sense of comfort that we get from holding on to old hurts. It is like marinating in your misery. Over time you develop a taste for agony and despair. Yet bathing in your own bitterness has a price tag because unforgiveness is a poison that rots the soul. It makes a person perpetually angry, bitter and a pain to be around. Unforgiveness also blocks our relationship with Christ because it flies in the face of Jesus' teaching that we forgive one another. In **Matthew 6:14**, the message is clear: **"For if you forgive other people when they sin against you, your heavenly Father will also forgive you."**

Forgiveness was my only way to get over it and get healed completely. Forgiveness meant suturing up the internal emotional wounds. Forgiveness did not disregard the harm that was done to me. It did free me from producing internal negatives that poisoned my soul. It also ended the painful dance in my mind that came from rehashing and rehearsing what was done to me. It liberated me from victimhood.

I read somewhere that there are lots of benefits of forgiveness. They were unproven, but I believed them. They were: accelerated healing, both emotionally and physically; relief from depression and resentment; increase in physical strength; stress reduction; immune system booster; better digestion, and a more positive outlook.

So I did it, but I could not do this alone. I placed the situations and the people who hurt me in the center of my mind and I said, "I forgive you all in the name of Jesus." I released all the energy and thoughts that were negative and replaced them with positive, and then I cried. The tears represented the water washing away the toxins. The water also washed away old emotions that were clutched tightly in my soul.

Now the healing began.

Now that my soul was healed, I was ready to return to helping others with my hands.

CHAPTER 17
Made By Hand

Handmade items have much more value for me. I am especially drawn to the handiwork of artisans and craftspeople who make jewelry encrusted with exotic beads, semi-precious stones. I seek tiny boutiques, trade fairs and art shows where artisans personally ply their wares. A creative high consumes me when I converse with artists about jewelry they have made. It is thrilling to have those imaginative hands place their necklace or bracelet on me. Making items by hand is very God-like because God is the ultimate creator. In the book of Genesis God's imagination created the world by hand.

The hands of those who have been healed have tremendous helping power as well. I built a house by hand with a cadre of other breast cancer survivors known as Breast Cancer Builds. A carpentry ministry underwrote the costs of the Habitat for Humanity project.

On a frigid February morning, nine months after my surgery, I stood in the frame of a house we were building with Habitat for Humanity and I thanked God for the journey. One year ago I was bargaining for my life by purchasing summer clothes. Now I was building for others via Habitat. Habitat for Humanity is a nonprofit, ecumenical Christian ministry founded on the conviction that every man, woman and child should have a decent, safe and affordable place to live.

Habitat has built more than 225,000 houses around the world since Millard Fuller and Linda Fuller founded it in 1976. This is a program that provides affordable houses that are actually built by volunteers and the homeowner.

This was the Breast Cancer Builds site, and we were happy to be alive. You could hear it in our voices and see it in our lively construction style. Thick, freezing mud was everywhere. The sun was barely up and yet my brave, bold cadre of women stood around sipping coffee before they went to work on our gratitude project. Soon came the loud grind of power saws, the thuds of hammers and the even louder laughs and cackles from my builders.

My body was healed. My breasts were like roses in bloom. Should I have returned back to my life as it was before?

No way! When someone gives you something, you must say thank you. I was humbled by my life. Now I needed to say thank you for letting me live. God does not scrimp or half- step. God gave vision to build homes with survivors, and provision came. Breast cancer survivors were easily and quickly recruited for Breast Cancer Builds. The media blasted the news of the building project and the survivors came running, like they were in the Boston marathon. God gave me an army of cancer survivors. There were men who made a difference with Breast Cancer Builds. One was Bob, husband of Linda, who was diagnosed in 1996. Bob stuck by her side during all the treatments and all the construction of the house too. Linda was the official coordinator of the volunteers and Bob was the unofficial comedian on-site. He kept us doubled over in laughter as we built and made the process a joy, not a chore.

We were a team of grateful hearts. We pounded nails into the frame of a house and sawed 2x4s, and hauled roof shingles around the building site. Not too long ago, some of us were in somebody's chemotherapy session or under a radiation machine receiving treatments or in an operating room. Breast cancer tried to take us out. Yet we lived.

For eight Saturdays we converged on a plot of land to construct the house, rain or shine. We enjoyed each other's company because we enjoyed being alive. Habitat for Humanity building projects pushed us beyond what we thought we could do. I could not spell "reticular saw," or use one prior to this experience. But I used the saw to cut out the frame for the windows in the front of the house. We were survivors and we refused to accept limitations and live cooped up. We boldly moved into new areas of life.

Why were we so tough? Surviving cancer turned us into brawlers of sorts. After you have won the war internally against the cancer cells, you were primed to fight anything else that got in your way. That's the way the other survivors felt too. We were a sisterhood of women who refused to cower to anything anymore. Like the wise woman builder in Proverbs 14:1 who built her own house. We understood the power God had given us.

We were contagious. There were other Habitat for Humanity houses being built around ours, and volunteers from other houses came over to hang out with us on Saturdays to soak us up.

Every Saturday was a fashion show of sorts, because some of the Breast Cancer Builders loved to bling in their own way with accessories and attitude. Personally, I spent my workdays in blue jeans, a pink BCB logo tee and matching bandanna. I was out-dressed every week and did not mind. There is enough bling to go around in this world.

Elaine, 65, was six years out of chemotherapy, but if you took one look at her hair you would think she was still in the midst of the treatment. Elaine's hair never quite returned. There was a smattering of short, uncooperative gray strands on her head. No worries ever came from her mouth. Elaine used the scant hair as a triumph. Every Saturday she wore a T-shirt that proclaimed, "I never have a bad hair day!" We treasured her humor. She showed up every Saturday ready to work and to make us laugh.

Candi, a nine-month breast cancer survivor, arrived every Saturday in a highly coordinated construction ensemble, pink gloves, pink tool belt and pink hammer. Candi was a sleek, athletic woman who participated in the Ironman marathons. She was so tough that her bout with breast cancer did not stop her from competing. Candi trained in between chemotherapy sessions. We went through our cancer at the same time. I admired her eagerness to use the power tools. Even though her slim frame shook like a rag doll when she used them, Candi never backed down from the opportunity to "let her rip."

K was the diva builder. She brought glamour in the midst of sawdust, mud and nails. Her long nails, stiletto boots, dangling gold earrings, multiple necklaces and suede pantsuit let everybody know that building a house and remaining stylish were not mutually exclusive. K's attire complimented her shiny bald head. She was still in the midst of chemotherapy, but her spunk level was sky high. K blessed us with her sassy spirit, and we blessed her too. She needed to spend time with others who had come out of the dark tunnel of breast cancer.

The woman and her two sons who would live in the house worked side by side with us. The family marveled at the reality that we were an all-women build team (a few men did help us) and that we all had battled cancer. "How is that possible?" they asked in amazement. We were probably not what they expected, a throng of women in pink, giddy at life and draped in blessing and bling. Week after week they watched us with caution that grew into admiration. When the house was completed the mother gave me a thank you card that said, "I don't know what I have ever done for God to send me such a group of strong women, but I am grateful. Working with this group has blessed me."

We were very strong together. As a team we made a statement to the world that in tough times we should not turn on each other, but reach out and hold the other up. I felt the strong bond of sisterhood like the one found in the book of Ruth. **"Don't urge me to leave you or turn back from you. Where you go, I will go, and where you stay I will stay. Your people will be my people and your God my God." Ruth 1:16**

A lot of people do not realize it, but those are words spoken between two women in the midst of travail, as they realized they needed each other to make it through tough times.

Breast Cancer Builds raised enough money for lots of mammograms. Now we needed to reach out to the masses.

CHAPTER 18

Fashion and Compassion

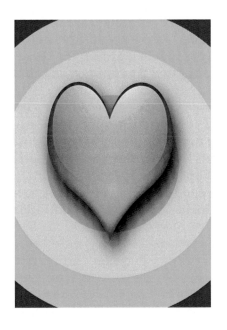

*Y*our level of fashion must match your level of compassion. Nothing is worse than a great dressing woman with an ice-cold heart. If you can reach out to a rack of clothes for the latest outfit, you must be able to reach out to someone in need as well. Fashion and compassion go hand-in-hand. Never, ever, would I permit my desire to style and profile to supersede a concern for those who go without basic human necessities. Helping others is another way I get high.

I admit it. One year after my surgery I was still high on helping people. I remained intoxicated with helping women stay healthy. Healthy people have lower rates of cancer and if they do contract the disease, they have a fighting chance of recovery. Lots of speaking invitations came and I took every one of them. I spread the blessings and bling around. I dubbed myself the "wellness advocate." It sounded good to me. I spoke at various women's events such as sorority luncheons, church worship services and corporate seminars.

My audiences were well-heeled, affluent women who came dressed to impress. Those with a true passion for fashion get thrills from wearing stylish clothes, but also observing other women's clothes. The suits, dresses, shoes and jewelry of my audiences were spectacular. Most importantly, the audiences were excited about my message. They pledged to take charge of their health, get annual mammograms and eat healthy. They enjoyed their gatherings whether it was over tuna salad and lemonade or Mimosas and chilled boiled shrimp. The laughter, girl talk and sisterly bonding were infectious. Usually, I bonded with the groups and had a hard time leaving the events. We would end with hugs and goodbyes and plans to get together and do it all again soon.

My blessings and bling took a sharp learning curve when I entered the world of women who were at low points in their lives. The funds raised from Breast Cancer Builds funded another program, Mammograms for the Masses and wheeled me into a second chance facility for women. The women there were ex-offenders, former drug and alcohol addicts, and formerly homeless. We raised enough money to underwrite the costs of a hospital's mobile mammogram unit to come and provide a two-day event with a breast health seminar and free mammograms. I was with them for two days. On the first day, I hosted a breast health seminar that included a motivational pep talk from me and sessions with experts on healthy eating and exercise. On the second day I hoped to personally escort them into the mammogram van that sat in the parking lot of their facility, so they could have access to the same preventive procedure that saved my life.

All eyes were on me as I rose to speak in a room filled with about 75 women on the first day. This was the place I was destined to be. This was new territory for me, but I was far from afraid. I realized that I had been waiting my whole life to bless them. God had intersected our lives. The cancer, the pain, the nonprofit, the program — all intersected right here. Thank you, God. I had never met these women, or they me, but they had been the target of my prayers for a long time. I just did not know it. This was what my breast cancer doctor told me about. God gave him a glimpse of this moment. What a moment it was. I was at the right place at the right time. This was Jesus' work. He said in **Matthew 25:40, "Whatever you did for one of the least of these brothers and sisters of mine, you did for me."**

I felt his spirit in that room. The ubiquitous question asks, "What would Jesus do?" He would be with us in this second chance center talking about breast health. I came to share my story with them, to encourage them in a healthy lifestyle, and offer them free mammograms paid for through the fruit of my loss. I thanked God for my loss. We gain by giving away. I thought that by losing my breasts I lost it all, but actually I gained the world. This moment proved it.

Surveying the group before me I was reminded that all of us go through something awful in our lives. No one is immune. It could be poverty, abandonment, incest, domestic violence, addictions, divorce, cancer and more. Even though all of us had been through something, we were all standing tall in that room. We were all testimonies of the power of God. I told them, "Ladies let's begin by giving God a hand clap of praise for the mere fact that we are still here. Hard times tried to take us out, but we are still here. God made a way out of no way and we are still here, standing tall and looking strong."

This group of women eyed me cautiously. This was a different crowd. Gone were the impressive clothes and designer shoes. These women were plainly dressed and their only accessories were traces of hard times etched on their faces. There was laughter, but it was different. They laughed to keep from crying.

One of the women in the group was Pat. Pat was the leader among the women. If I persuaded her to get a mammogram, the rest would follow. I was there to help them. As it turned out, they helped me. Pat and her co-workers took me to the proverbial school of hard knocks those two days. I learned that there are horrific factors in women's lives that affect their decisions about health. And no one should judge them. Especially me.

"I just don't want any more bad news," Pat said to me when I asked her if she wanted to get a mammogram.

"White liquid leaks from my breast whenever it brushes against something," she explained calmly. Pat was unruffled about this situation because that was the way it was. Period. Her face showed the fear she kept balled up inside until she found someone who cared and could help her. I asked, "How long has it been this way, and why haven't you gotten any help?"

All Pat could do was to repeat her previous statement, "I just don't want any more bad news."

Her simple request for no more bad news was actually complicated. Pat's life had been a series of bad news. A former crack addict, Pat spent seven years in prison. During those years, she explained that her son, "had to raise himself" because she was not there. Now that she was out of prison they had a hard time bonding. On top of that she had another major illness and had trouble paying for the medication. Pat did not need any more bad news. A mammogram that brought news of more disease was not what she needed. Who was I to tell her she needed it?

As I drove home from the center that day, I decided that I would not blame Pat if she declined the mammogram. I would not blame the other women that Pat worked with if they declined too. Their lives were not picnics either. Everyone deserved the right to prioritize their problems. The women at this center did not need me to come and stir up more trouble. I accepted the fact that promoting health can create more problems for some. This was a sobering realization.

I tossed and turned all night long. The next day, when I walked into the mobile unit, the first face I saw was Pat's. I was elated. She was proud of her bravery too. Pat's medical situation was so advanced that she was immediately referred to a hospital. Still, coming to the mammogram van was a reason to celebrate. Many of the women Pat influenced came for mammograms as well.

I left the second chance center clear on two things: a need for sensitivity and a need to increase my reach. Working with women who struggle for the basics of life made me aware of how I presented my wellness advocacy. Being someone else's blessing means understanding and recognizing where they are. Sometimes I needed to curb my enthusiasm. All women are not enthusiastic about their health. Health is a luxury for some. Some women struggle with loving themselves, and taking care of themselves is an act of love they are not ready to commit. Sometimes women have more pressing concerns like where they will sleep that night, and if they will eat or not. Their health is not something that registers as vital.

I kept high hope for the women of the center and all women who find themselves in tough situations. Just because a woman was down today, does not mean she will be down forever. All things are possible, and they can get their lives on track and become women with the gleam and glow of accomplishment and achievement.

I left that center clear on something else. God was not done using me to bless others. The invitations kept coming and I kept saying yes. I was reaching out all over the place and eventually my blinging reach went global.

CHAPTER 19

Global Glamour

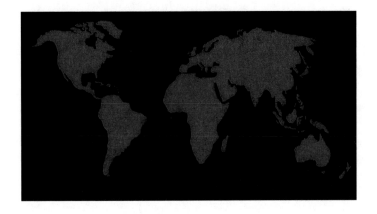

Women all over the world work at looking good. Whether they are in a humble hut or a grandiose palace, women seek and attain beauty that is recognized in their own land. That is a beautiful fact about women; glamour is in our blood. For example in parts of western Africa such as Mauritania, women are considered attractive when they are overweight. Young women aspire to plump up to a catch the eyes of a young man. The Tibeto-Burman women of Burma wear brass coils around their necks to give the appearance that their necks are growing. The long, towering necks are status symbols.

I saw global glamour up close and personal when I spent time with international delegations of breast cancer survivors and breast cancer nurses and physicians from the Middle East and North Africa. The 17-person delegation visited the United States as guests of the U.S. Department of State's International Visitor Leadership Program in partnership with the World Learning and the World Affairs Council of Dallas/ Fort Worth. Representing countries such as Bahrain, Syria, Libya and Egypt, they taught me that I did not have a patent on blessing or bling. They also had been rescued from breast cancer. They wanted to do something about it, but they did not know how. Their visit to the US included meetings with high-profile breast cancer awareness advocates, tours of hospitals, cancer facilities and a meeting with me. It was an honor to have access to the group. It would not have mattered how they looked, but the beauty of these women was riveting, as were their stories of overcoming cancer. After an hour with them, I would never be the same.

I stood in the doorway of their hotel and watched their bus arrive. They had spent the day touring and I was the last appointment of the day. They exited their bus and I gasped as a stream of international women headed in my direction. Some were wrapped in exotic fabrics from head to toe, as if they just stepped off the streets of their native lands. Others were dressed in smart suits and looked very Western. Some were fair-skinned and some were brown-skinned like me. All possessed a beauty that comes from a woman who empties herself for others. And they were all coming to visit with me. They complimented my outfit and I complimented theirs. We bonded over the bling.

We sat and talked in the hotel lobby and created a breast cancer sisterhood that transcended borders, language and politics. They were hungry for dialogue. They all wanted to tell their stories. They all wanted to be heard. Whether through a translator, broken or impeccable English, they talked freely and joyously. Many of them are denied the luxury of talking about breast cancer in their countries because it carries a stigma like the HIV virus AIDS.

"Women don't talk about this," I was told. "They have breast cancer, and they choose to die quietly because the culture says they did something wrong to get it. When women die of it, their obituaries say they died of a long illness."

A 52-year-old breast cancer survivor from Syria offered a story of activism. Once her doctor discovered her breast cancer, and she had a mastectomy, she went on to organize mobile mammograms in her country.

A physician from Libya told a painful story. "There is a social stigma in my country. Women deny breast cancer until it is too late. Breast cancer is a scary disease. There is no advocacy or media support. There are no breast cancer care centers, and there is a shortage of medicine. We are lagging behind, and we should give a hand to women."

A doctor from the Sultanate of Oman is a survivor and a member of the National Cancer Association. Hers was a story of denial and eventual acceptance.

"Years ago, I was not aware of what breast cancer was. I was examined and breast cancer was found, but I told the doctor that I was not sick, and I left the hospital. They came for me and took me back to the hospital.

"Eventually, I had a double mastectomy. Women are not afraid of dying," she said. "They are afraid of losing their breasts. Unless you have a good system of friends and family, you will feel bad during this time. Being a woman without breasts is a terrible life."

Breast cancer presents other challenges to their cultures.

Women prefer women doctors, and that is not always possible. They do not feel comfortable going to male doctors and having their breasts examined. It can be difficult to educate women on breast health, especially when the women have little formal education. One health care worker shared what happened when she spoke in a rural area of her country about the connection between proper diet and breast health. "One woman stood up and said, "How does the mouth hurt the breast?"

We laughed together and cried together in mutual happiness to have survived breast cancer. "How can we do what you are doing for women and breast cancer?" one woman asked me.

"The fact that you traveled all the way to the US is a major sign that you are dedicated to helping others," I said. "Never forget that you survived breast cancer for a reason. You have been spared to help another woman. Spread the word, tell your stories, and keep on looking good while you do it."

Not only was I reaching out. I was sprouting out. It was a good thing.

Blessings and bling across continents was further proof that God was still in the midst of my journey.

CHAPTER 20

New Lingerie, New Life

The leopard print padded, the midnight purple push-up, the emerald green demi, the cherry red strapless and the magenta underwire bras all hung from their racks and called my name in unison. This time I stopped and heeded their calls. I purchased them all. I am ending this journey, where you met me, in a store. I am shopping again, but this time I am not shopping to save my life. I am shopping for new bras and new life. The breast cancer is behind me and I pray daily that it does not return. I am sprinting ahead for what God has for me.

My old bras do not fit anymore. I went from a 34 B to a 36 DD with the help of my gorgeous plastic surgeon and his team. They completed the final follow-up surgeries for my breast augmentation and my profile has, shall we say, changed. It was a long, painstaking journey, but who would complain about something like that? After the chest expanders stretched out my muscles and skin, surgery was performed to remove the expanders and insert saline implants. Months later my plastic surgeon created nipples on the breasts he expertly constructed. It was a feat to behold. He took thread and with the precision and skill of a couture seamstress gathered skin to fashion very attractive nipples.

I tried on my old, *before cancer* bras. I had outgrown them. So I tossed them out. Never try to cram newness into something old. It will not work. The new, *after cancer* bras in my shopping bags also illustrate my new life. They are larger with more space and capacity for what God has given me. I tried to go back to my life before cancer. It did not fit anymore. I had outgrown it, so I tossed my old ways of doing and got some new ways. Cancer changed me dramatically from the inside out, and I am grateful to God for the opportunity to be changed for the better.

I feel closer to God.

I do not fear death.

I do not fear hospitals, needles or surgery.

I am more patient with myself and others.

I see God's handiwork more readily.

I want more women to get healthy and stay healthy

Isaiah the prophet wrote: "I am doing a new thing. Can you not see it, it springs forth now?" I see what God has done and I applaud it. I have the audacity to say, I thank God for my cancer. The journey has been amazing.

I want new, bountiful and overflowing life for you too. God has blessings for us all. You deserve everything God has for you.

I have shared the raw truth of my experience in hopes that it will empower, inspire and educate you. It would be easy to pretend I never had a bad day following my diagnosis or to act as if, because I am a pastor or because I have a relationship with Christ, that I never faltered. But maintaining that illusion of control would not help you. If you're someone facing cancer, you have enough to deal with now. You don't need the added pressure of feeling as if you can't be honest about your emotions.

I went through so many emotions over the course of finding out about my diagnosis and the treatment. What I realized is that honestly acknowledging how I was feeling led to my spiritual healing. And I believe taking care of our emotional issues can play a part in our physical healing, too. So don't be afraid to acknowledge how you feel — no matter who you are. It doesn't matter if you are a housewife, a CEO of a large company, the pastor of a congregation, a wife, a mother, a daughter or a sister. You are entitled to your feelings. No one can tell you how to feel.

Once you acknowledge the feelings, find a way to address them. I told you that I went to a practitioner of Eastern medicine and she helped me discover that unforgiveness was holding me back. Choose someone who can help you heal, as well.

And look for a project that will help you make sense of your diagnosis and will allow you to help others. It doesn't have to be big. Just find something you are interested in doing that also allows you to plan for the future and help someone else. This is helpful for several reasons. One, it can give you something else to focus on as you face your cancer battle. Having something other than your diagnosis can lift your spirits and give you an outlet. Two, this project can allow you to put the attention on something positive going on in your life, rather than allowing dark feelings to consume your every waking thought. The projects I created really helped me — emotionally and spiritually.

A third reason for finding a project is that it can give you new purpose. When I worked on the projects I told you about — whether it was building a Habitat House for a needy family or raising money for mammograms — the work energized me.

Even as you become involved in a new project, remember to keep it in perspective. Don't put undue pressure on yourself to be perfect or to make unrealistic goals. If you miss a meeting or an event because you were a little tired or didn't quite feel up to it, don't beat yourself up over it. Your project is there to help you on your journey, not burden you with additional pressure. Assemble a team of people to help you. They can take up the slack when you need to sit down and rest.

The whole theme of this book has been blessings and bling. Many may wonder why I chose to focus on bling — or fashion and looking good — while dealing with such a serious matter. I hope after reading this book, you understand the reason for that, but I will reiterate it here briefly: Looking good can help you feel good. There were many days when I did not feel great when I woke up, but once I got dressed in a beautiful outfit, I felt a little bit better. In a cancer fight, we take every advantage we can, and if some nice clothes — some bling — will help, we certainly will take that, too. Find the thing that works for you.

The Blessings and Bling Cancer Survival Guide

Here are a few keys that truly helped me as I faced my cancer battle. Consider how they can help you:

1. Acknowledge your emotions.
Complete the following sentence. Today, I feel

_____.

Embrace whatever comes with this acknowledgment.

2. Talk honestly with God.
God is there for us at every turn. If you are scared, nervous or even angry, it is okay to talk to God about it. It's all right to be honest. God wants to have open communication with us. When you talk with God, spend some time quietly listening for answers to your questions and concerns. Write a brief note to God, revealing what's going on with you. You may consider journaling to God. Get a bound journal or simple notebook and begin to write out what you feel. Journaling is a very positive way to relate and release to God. It is also an amazing way to track the blessings that come into your life.

_____

_____

_____

3. Spend some time on spiritual matters.
A cancer diagnosis can bring with it chaos and confusion. If you're like me, you might even go through a period of stepping away from prayer and God. But be open to returning to a relationship with God. Even in the midst of your confusion

and anger, set aside some time for prayer, meditation, Bible study and fasting. Write down a favorite scripture here, and think about what it means as you face cancer.

_____

_____

_____

You do not have to be a prayer warrior or fasting expert; do your best.

If you are a member of a faith community, keep attending worship services. There is undeniable power in the pews as the Word of God is preached. If you do not choose to attend worship, get your Word via pod cast, DVD or television. Remember **Romans 10:17** says, **"Faith comes from hearing the message, and the message is heard through the word about Christ."**

4. Gather a support system.

Your support system may be close family and friends. Or you may find the need to look elsewhere. The main thing is to have a support system. Cancer is not something to face alone. Join a prayer group, a cancer support group, an organization of survivors, or some other collection of people who can share experiences with you and with whom you can share your experiences.

Write down the names of at least two people you can talk with about what is going on in your life right now. If you cannot write down the names of individuals, write down the name and contact information for at least one group you can seek out and join:

_____.

_____.

Now, make contact with at least one person on the list or

the group you wrote about — within the next 24 hours. If you make contact with a friend or family member, schedule some time in the coming days to chat, have lunch, visit or engage in some way.

If you make contact with a group, find out when the next meeting is scheduled and make plans to attend.

5. Get a project.

A project will give you something else to focus on and will also give you new purpose. Projects develop our capacity to care about others despite our situations. Often personal trauma like cancer tries to make us turn inward and focus solely on self. That is not God's will for you. Write down three or four ideas you have for helping others or three or four organizations you are interested in checking out.

_____.

_____.

_____.

_____.

Now investigate these options within the next two weeks and see if any will be a good fit for you.

6. Embrace your choices.

You will have several decisions to make over the course of your cancer battle. Make the choices you feel are best for you, and do not allow others' lack of understanding, information or empathy to make you feel bad about what you are doing for you. When I chose to have a double mastectomy, some people could not see why I was doing it. Some even thought it was unnecessary for me to remove both breasts when only one had cancer. But my health choices were not about pleasing them. They were about protecting me. Choose to protect you.

Get educated about your cancer and your options. Request pamphlets and brochures from your doctor's office, look up reputable related websites and seek out educational organizations.

Choose to be an empowered and informed person who is involved in her treatment. If you are uninsured or underinsured, look for information about programs that will help reduce or cover costs for treatment. You can research this information with community organizations, social service agencies, health agencies, churches and others.

Keep a notebook of the information you find. Decide which are the best options for you.

7. Get active or remain active.

Do not allow a cancer diagnosis to keep you from working out and moving around. Exercise is one of the best ways to take your mind off of your trouble. Just sitting around collecting dust, does not do your body any good. It could be a brisk walk around the block or taking the stairs to your doctor's office rather than the elevator.

I am partial to yoga. It is easy on the joints and very peaceful and calm. The slow breathing exercises help me center and focus on what is important. When I practice it, my mind is clearer and my body is humming.

This ancient practice from India is the subject of recent medical studies that found women with breast cancer who practiced yoga experienced higher levels of happiness, better skills for coping with the disease and an improved quality of life.

8. Monitor what goes into your mouth.

Just because you have cancer, you cannot eat anything you want. You still need to eat sensibly. Eat like you know you have a long, fabulous life ahead of you! I am telling you what I hope you already know. The basics: Drink at least 8 glasses of water each day; eat fresh fruits and vegetables at each meal, if possible; avoid fatty, fried foods.

I eliminated red meat from my diet 10 years ago and do

not miss it at all.

Every few months consider going on a raw food cleanse. No, you do not have to buy anything special, just fruits, veggies and herbal teas. This cleanse gives your digestive system a clean sweep and a rest. Eliminate salt, sugar, caffeine and processed food from your diet for a week. Your body will thank you.

9. Get you some bling!

Get a couple of cute pieces of clothing. This doesn' t have to be a budget buster. Whether you shop at trendy boutiques or find great deals at your local thrift shop or consignment store, choose to get a couple of items to make you feel good. These can be clothes you wear on days when you don't feel like doing much, or they can be items you pick out to wear in the next season.

•

Well, that's enough from me, for now. I'm about to head out of this store with my new bras. But as soon as I turn to go, a lace bra with rhinestones whispers my name.

Here we go again!

About the Author

Dr. Sheron C. Patterson is a grateful breast cancer survivor who believes in helping others survive on a national and an international basis. In 2006, Dr. Patterson was diagnosed with breast cancer. She turned what could have been a tragedy into a triumph by creating numerous wellness and breast cancer awareness programs that touched thousands.

As a result, "The Patterson Pledge," "Mammograms for the Masses" and "Breast Cancer Builds" were created.

Whether she hosts international delegations of breast cancer survivors or encourages women who live in homeless shelters, Dr. Patterson has a message that lifts persons from all walks of life.

Dr. Sheron C. Patterson is an author of eight books that empower and encourage women. She has amassed an impressive 20 years as a radio and television host. She has been featured on CNN and BET. She is an ordained United Methodist pastor with twenty years as senior pastor. She holds degrees from Spelman College and Southern Methodist University's Perkins School of Theology. A native of Charlotte, North Carolina, she is a wife and the mother of two sons.

Would you like to get another copy of this book for a friend?

Additional copies of The Blessing and Bling are available on Amazon.com